More Table Tennis Tips

Three More Years and 150 More Online Tips
All in One Volume

By Larry Hodges
TableTennisCoaching.com
U.S. Table Tennis Hall of Famer and National Coach
©2017, v03-15-17

Back Cover
Photo of Larry Hodges by Wen Hsu
at the Maryland Table Tennis Center,
ITTF Hopes Camp, March, 2017

TABLE OF CONTENTS

CHAPTER THREE: STROKES

General

Power

Forehand

Looping

Blocking and Defense

Pushing

CHAPTER FOUR: FOOTWORK AND READY POSITION

CHAPTER FIVE: TACTICS

CHAPTER SIX: IMPROVING

General

Your Game

Practice

FOREWORD

Welcome, fellow table tennis fanatics, to *another* three years' worth of Tips of the Week, compiled in one volume in logical progression. This book is a follow-up and companion piece to my previous book, *Table Tennis Tips*, which covered the 150 Tips of the Week I put up from January, 2011 through December 2013. This volume covers the next 150, from January 2014 through December 2016. (It also goes well with *Table Tennis Tactics for Thinkers*, my best-selling table tennis book.)

These Tips are online, available for free to anyone. I put them up every Monday on my website, TableTennisCoaching.com. Feel free to browse them—but do you really want to have to call them up, one by one, in random order as far as content goes? I've updated quite a few of them here, not to mention a lot of editing. Some had links to specific online videos, so I had to adjust the wording, inviting readers to go to YouTube.com and put in the specific URLs or do basic searches.

The tips in this volume range over nine basic topics: Serving, Receiving, Strokes, Footwork and Ready Position, Tactics, How to Improve, Sports Psychology, Equipment, and Tournaments.

There are unavoidable redundancies. The content of the Tips often overlap with other Tips. This is unavoidable as many of the Tips cover parallel material. For example, there are two Tips here on Controlling a Match. I didn't even realized I'd used the same title twice until I began putting this volume together – but while they cover similar topics, the Tips do so in different fashion. I put them back to back for readers to get both perspectives.

I'd like to thank the "Terrific Trio" who proofed the book for me, pointing out numerous problems, from typos and grammar mistakes to better wording suggestions. They did an incredible job of making me look good. They are:

- **Mark Dekeyser**
- **John Olsen**
- **Dennis Taylor**

CHAPTER ONE: SERVE

GENERAL

January 11, 2016 – What Is a Good Serve?

Ask ten people, and you might get ten answers. But there is a simple definition: a Good Serve is one that helps you win. Ideally, this would mean a serve that the other guy can't return – but if you can do that, your opponent isn't your level anyway. What you really want is a serve that sets up Your Game.

This means that if your best shot is a loop, then your serve should set up your loop as often as possible. If your best shot is a smash, then that's what your serve should set up. If you are more of a counterdriver, then that's what you want the serve to set up. And so on. On the other hand, what's a good serve for one player might not be a good serve for another. A short backspin serve might set up a looper who wants a push return – but it might not set up a counterdriver, who wants to get into a topspin-countering rally. A fast & deep serve might set up a hitter or counterdriver, but it might take a looper's best shot away. This doesn't mean a player should always serve the same way – but that they should favor the serves that will set them up for their best shot.

You also have to take the future into account. If you are a blocker, you might win now by serving long over and over and letting your opponent attack so you can block. And while that might not be a bad tactic, strategically you might want to learn to serve and attack, perhaps by serving short, so you can add another aspect to your game. So you might want to develop serves that set you up to play the way you want to win in the future.

So develop lots of Good Serves, which set up your game now, in the future . . . or perhaps ones that just win you points directly from the sheer Goodness of the Serve.

August 18, 2014 – The Purpose of the Serve

The serve is one of the most misunderstood techniques in table tennis. Many players serve just to get the ball in play, or to keep the opponent from attacking, or to try to score winners with every serve. So what is the purpose of the serve?

The primary purpose of the serve is to set up your attack. Unless the receiver does something to stop your attack, you should serve and attack essentially every time you serve. This doesn't mean your first attack has to be a winner, but it should be aggressive.

In the modern game, attacking usually means looping, either forehand or backhand. Most favor the usually more powerful forehand, but others loop from either side, depending on where the receive is, and some may favor the backhand loop. Others use the serve to set up their smash, either with a serve and smash, or a serve to set up a loop, and the loop to set up the smash. (This is rare at the higher levels, where looping completely dominates, but is still common at the intermediate level.)

This doesn't mean you don't sometimes serve for winners. In fact, players who do not have any "trick" serves that are designed to trick an opponent into an easy miss are lacking in their service game. (Trick serves usually only work a few times, however.) Most serves should be used to set up the attack. Even if the serve is a trick serve where you hope the opponent will miss the serve outright, you should assume it's coming back, and be ready for the follow-up, which should be an attack unless the opponent does something to stop it. If anything, you should be so expecting your "trick" serves to come back that when an opponent misses it, you are surprised as you were so waiting to follow up with an attack.

Even defensive players should use the serve to set up an attack, even if it's only an occasional one. For example, the defensive player may serve and look for a specific return (or just a generally weak one), and if he gets it, attack. If he doesn't, then he may go back on defense.

Some players may use the serve to set up their best rallying shot. For example, a blocker might serve long, and then quick-block the next ball. Or a counter-hitter might serve short topspin, which brings the receiver in over the table while starting a topspin rally, and then the server can get right into aggressive counter-hitting, with the receiver perhaps jammed to the table and so unable to start the rally off well.

Once you get into the mindset that the purpose of the serve is to set up your attack, then you can begin to gain experience on which serves set up which returns, and how and where to best attack them. Once you have this serve and attack mind-set, you'll soon be dominating the points on your serve. We'll finish with an acronym that I just made up and that's a bit dated for the pre-looping years (when hitting dominated), but always remember to "**S**erve and **M**ake **A S**trong **H**it" – SMASH!

August 11, 2014 – Ten Steps to a Great Service Game

1. Learn to serve with lots of spin by accelerating the racket through the ball and grazing it.
2. Learn to serve various spins, including backspin, side-backspin, sidespin, side-topspin, and topspin, and be able to serve with sidespin in either direction.
3. Learn to serve low to the net.
4. Learn to control the depth and direction of the serve.
5. Learn to serve with spin using a semi-circular motion so you can create different spins with the same motion by varying where in the motion you contact the ball.
6. Learn to minimize and do quickly this semi-circular motion so the receiver has trouble picking up contact.
7. Learn to change the direction of your follow-through with your racket the split second after contact to mislead the receiver.
8. Learn to fake spin and serve no-spin by contacting the ball near the handle.
9. Learn to serve fast & deep as a variation to your spin serves.
10. Learn to follow up your serves.

January 27, 2014 – Practicing Serves the Productive Way

It's almost a cliché. I hand someone a box of balls to practice their serves. Then grab a ball and serve, grab a ball and serve, grab a ball and serve, and so on, all done with the speed and thoughtfulness of firing a machine gun. Then they wonder why their serves aren't any good. There's a lot more to developing great serves than rapid-fire serve practice, where the goal seems to be to empty the box of balls as rapidly as possible. So what should you do differently?

First and foremost, learn the proper way to execute great serves. You can do this by watching players with great serves, or a coach or top player can show you. It's pointless to practice your serves if you don't know how to do them properly.

Once you have at least some idea of what you need to practice, get that box of balls and go to the table. It's generally best done alone; having someone return your serve can be a distraction, especially when you are learning a new serve. (But sometimes you want someone to return your serves, so you can get feedback, and to see how much difficulty they have.)

Grab a ball and get ready to start. You might want to first hold a ball in your fingers (tightly) and practice the actual contact you are going to make with the ball. (But don't rub the sponge into the held ball too hard or you'll damage your sponge.)

Now go into your serving position, and come to a complete stop. The rules actually state that you must start the serve with the ball resting freely on the palm of your *stationary* free hand--but there's a more important reason to do this than complying with the rules.

This is where you visualize the serve in your head. Don't just grab a ball and mechanically serve it; from now on, never serve a ball without first seeing it done exactly as you want it done, in your head. This is what the top players do. Visualization is one of the best tools in sports, and for serving, it's especially good since there are no outside influences--it's just you and the ball. In your head, see how you swing at the ball, the contact, and the entire trajectory of the serve as you want it to go.

After you've visualized the serve in your head, go ahead and serve. Don't try to guide it; let the subconscious take over. (You should do this for all table tennis shots.) Let go; it's as if you're just an observer. Watch the ball as it leaves your racket. Did it bounce on each side of the table at the spot as you visualized? Did it bounce low to the net as you visualized? Did it go at the speed you visualized? Did it have the spin you visualized? Did it go short or long as you visualized? Am I emphasizing the word *visualize* enough for you to make clear its importance?

Now visualize the next serve, making corrections for what went wrong in the previous one, and emphasizing the aspects that went right. You are now well on your way to developing great serves. You should also be tired and sweaty pretty soon--serving is a very physical motion. You can't make the ball spin at extremely high speeds if you can't get your racket moving at extremely high speeds, like a whip.

Does any of this sound boring? It shouldn't. If you just grab a ball and serve, grab a ball and serve, grab a ball and serve, that's like working an assembly line at a factory. *That's boring.* But serving is the trick part of table tennis, and practicing your serves, and all the tricky, deceptive things you can do with them, while revving up and varying the spin, is like practicing a magic trick. That's not boring, and neither should practicing serves.

March 21, 2016 – Visualize Your Serves and Make Them Do Tricks

Before you serve you should always visualize what the ball is going to do. It amazes me how many players just serve without really doing this. Top players have practiced their serves so much that this is instinctive – they don't think about it, they just know exactly what the ball is going to do. Visualizing a serve means seeing in your head before you serve the contact, direction, speed, spin, height, depth, bounces, and curve of the ball.

One fun way of practicing this is to make your serves do tricks. For example, try serving backspin where you graze the ball so finely that all your energy goes into backspin – and so the serve bounces backward into the net. But it's not enough for the ball to come backwards – you should be able to visualize its actual path in advance. Try serving where you visualize how deep the ball will go and how many bounces before it comes backwards, and the direction it'll come back (since most backspin serves have some sidespin as well). This visualizing includes what the ball does on your side of the net – how fast the ball will travel, where the first bounce on your side will be, and how low to the net it'll be. (When first practicing heavy backspin serves or trying to make the ball bounce backwards, don't worry about serving too low. But as you master the serve, you want the ball to practically skim the net.)

Serving backspin so that the ball bounces back into the net isn't really a serve you need in a match. In fact, it's better to drive such a backspin serve out more so that the second bounce is near the end-line, making it difficult for the receiver to attack, push short, or rush you with a quick, deep push. But the key is being able to control the serve – and you can't control it unless you know what you want the ball to do. Try to visualize the entire path of the ball in advance, including both bounces on the far side, and the way the ball curves between bounces if there's sidespin.

Do the same with a regular sidespin serve, where you serve to one side of the table, but curve it back to the other side – but visualize the curving path of the ball in advance. Perhaps set up a target (improvise) and try to curve the ball into the target.

Then do the same thing with your deep serves, perhaps putting up targets on the far end-line, and try to hit them – again, visualizing the entire path of the ball in advance, right up until it smacks the target. Then do the same with all your other serves, with or without targets.

At first, this visualizing will feel like a hassle that slows you down. But soon it'll become second nature, and you won't even think about it – but you'll have master control over your serves.

April 13, 2015 – How Many Serving Motions Should You Have?

If you watch the top players you'll notice that most have only one or two basic serving motions that they use over and over. The majority just do forehand pendulum and reverse pendulum serves. This allows them to do every possible type of spin, including sidespin both ways. Most have a few "trick" serves they'll pull out sometimes, but the large majority of their serves are almost relentlessly the same few motions, though the spins vary quite a bit.

But they are world-class players playing other world-class players, who are not particularly vulnerable to trick serves or varying service motions. That's not true of the large majority of players. Against them, you should also have only one or two basic serving motions that you use most of the time. But you will have a huge advantage if you can regularly pull out other serving motions, as long as you can do them *effectively*.

After a game or two, most players adjust to an opponent's serving motion. But what if you are able to pull out other ones, and keep them guessing? For example, after a few forehand pendulum (or regular or reverse), throw in a backhand serve, or tomahawk serve, or any of a zillion other possibilities. The key is not to just throw out these serves as

13

just "trick" serves, but actually learn to do them well. Otherwise they are one-serve wonders, which have value if used perhaps one time, but not much beyond that. Instead, develop these other serves so you can pull them out a few times each game, and perhaps get a few "easy" points.

It takes a lot of practice to develop multiple serving motions, and just as much time getting comfortable using them in games (where you not only can do the serves, but get used to the various returns). It's a lot of work for a seemingly small return. But is it really a small return? Players spend years improving parts of their games only marginally. Perfect a new serving motion, and you may find opponents struggling against your serves later and later into games, including those all-important points near the end of a close game.

April 20, 2015 – Visualize Serves for Feedback

When you serve, whether in a match or when practicing, you should always first visualize the serve in your mind. You should see the serve's entire path and everything it does before serving – the contact off your racket, its speed and spin, the first bounce, its path over the net (low, any curving due to spin), the second bounce on the far side, and where it bounces after that. You should also feel the contact in your head, whether a grazing contact to create great spin or sinking more into the sponge for more speed.

Then serve, and observe if the reality matches what was in your mind. This gives feedback so that you can learn to control and develop the serve. Most players who have trouble controlling their serve (i.e. most) do not use this feedback, and so it's no surprise they can't control their serve. This also allows you to improve the serve by visualizing as it should be, and striving to match that.

When practicing, perhaps play a game with yourself where you visualize different serves, and see if you can match what's in your head. Practice until you can do this with all of your serves, including both spin serves and fast, deep serves. Perhaps even put targets on the table and visualize hitting them, and then do so. Eventually you'll have the feel of any serve you can visualize in your head, and to repeat that serve you just have to match the feel of the serve that you've learned.

May 16, 2016 – Depth Control on Serves with CBS

When trying to serve shorter, many players slow down their swing, and when trying to serve long they speed up their swing. Both are mistakes – that's *not* how you should control depth or even ball speed.

"Serving is a violent motion," said two-time (and soon to be five-time) U.S. Men's Champion and future long-time U.S. Men's Team Coach Dan Seemiller at a training camp in the late 1970s – and those words have always stuck with me. If you want to maximize the spin, you maximize the racket speed. (You do this with smooth acceleration, but that's another topic.) If you want to maximize the speed, you also maximize the racket speed (at least as fast as you can make it and keep it on the table).

So how do you adjust the depth? Not by changing the racket speed, which should always reach a maximum around contact, but by three things: the grazing contact; where the ball bounces on your side of the table; and the spin.

If you barely graze the ball, you get two things: more spin and less speed. This means a shorter serve (i.e. one that would likely bounce two or more times on the far side if given the chance). As you sink the ball a bit more into the sponge, you get more speed and so the ball goes deeper. You also lose a little spin – though not as much as you'd think. More of your energy now goes into speed and so you lose some spin, but you also gain some spin from the rebounding of the sponge, since you've sunk the ball slightly into it at an angle.

And so you can control the depth primarily by how much you graze the ball. Want it to go short? Graze it finely (and get more spin as well), and the ball will travel slower, and so land shorter. Want it to go longer? Sink it a bit more into the sponge.

You also control depth by where it bounces on your side of the table. If the first bounce is near the net, you'll tend to get a shorter serve. If it's nearer your own end-line, then the ball has a long way to go to get to the net – 4.5 feet – and so will likely bounce deeper. Most top players like to serve the ball so the first bounce is as close to their own end-line as possible while still barely going short (with the second bounce on the far side, given the chance, right on the end-line or sometimes just a touch past it).

You also control depth with spin – backspin will make it bounce shorter, topspin longer. A good sidespin serve can also make the ball go shorter as it curves the ball sideways, keeping it over the table rather than bouncing out.

You also can keep the ball shorter by serving it low over the net – but that's a given. *Always* serve low to the net. You also can get a "shorter" serve by serving crosscourt, where you have more table, instead of down the line.

So learn to serve with that "violent" motion, and vary the depth with your contact, first bounce, and spin. It's easy to remember – Contact, Bounce, Spin = CBS! (After practicing your serves, you have my permission to go watch TV.)

November 24, 2014 – Pre-Serve Routine – a 1-2-3 Approach

Many players serve without any type of routine. They just go to the table, decide what serve to do, and then serve. If all you want to do is get the ball in play, that's fine. But if you want to serve effectively, there's more to it.

First, you need to mentally prepare yourself for each serve. That means going through a pre-serve routine. It can be short and simple, such as just coming to a complete stop (as required by the serving rules), where you finalize what serve you will do, and then clear your mind to prepare for the upcoming rally. Or it could be a bit more. Some bounce the ball on the table or even the floor. Others wipe their hand on the table. I like to push up the sleeve of my serving shoulder, drop my serving arm so it hangs loosely, and then swing it back and forth one time like a pendulum (which also helps loosen the arm muscles). Then I come to a complete stop, visualize the serve, and then serve it. (I decide what the serve will be before I start this routine, though I often change my mind afterwards while visualizing the serve.)

Second, you need to visualize the serve. That means all aspects of it:

1. **Height of toss** - here's a Tip on Height of Service Toss:

www.tabletenniscoaching.com/node/1595

2. **Height of contact** (low!)
3. **Location of contact** - here's a Tip on Service Contact Point: www.tabletenniscoaching.com/node/1589
4. **Speed of contact**
5. **Contact itself** (grazing for spin, flatter for speed); here's a Tip on Five Steps to a Great Spin Serve: www.tabletenniscoaching.com/node/1524
6. **Direction of the serve** - here's are Tips on Where to Serve Short, and on Turn Opponents Into Puppets with Long Serves: www.tabletenniscoaching.com/node/1607 www.tabletenniscoaching.com/node/1125
7. **Flight of the ball** (curving if there is sidespin, sinking if topspin, floating if backspin)
8. **Location of first bounce** (where on your side of table)
9. **Break on first bounce** (if a spin serve)
10. **Where it crosses the net** (always low); here's a Tip on Serving Low: www.tabletenniscoaching.com/node/951
11. **Location of second bounce** (where on table, both direction and depth); here's a Tip on Depth Control of Serves: www.tabletenniscoaching.com/node/697
12. **Height of bounce on far side** - See Tip on Serving Low (#10 above)
13. **Break on second bounce** (if a spin serve)

Does this mean going through a checklist of all of the above? NO!!! It means visualizing all aspects of the serve, taken as a whole. You can recognize a person's face without consciously noticing what makes it different from another's. Similarly, you can visualize an entire serve without consciously noting each aspect.

Third, you have to be ready for the follow-up. This means getting into a proper ready stance immediately after the serve. It also means mentally being ready to follow up the serve. This has to be a flexible approach – never force something that isn't there. For example, you might decide you are looking to follow your serve with a forehand loop. If the opponent pushes and you are able to get to it, you get to make your shot. But if your opponent attacks the serve, drops it short, or catches you off guard with an aggressive push that you can't get your forehand on, you need to flexibly react to that shot. Similarly, a player may decide he's going to follow with a loop from either side, depending on where the ball goes – but if the opponent drops the ball short, you have to flexibly change your shot.

This last aspect takes experience to get right. For example, if an opponent pushes your serve back over and over, an experienced player may decide to use the following tactic: when he serves backspin, he'll likely get a heavier, lower return, and so follow with forehand or backhand loop, depending on where the ball goes. But if he serves no-spin, he'll likely get a lighter, higher return, and so look to follow with a forehand. (I do this tactic all the time.) In theory, this makes it look like you should serve more no-spin, but there's also a higher probability that it'll be attacked, plus you need to vary the serve so the opponent can't get used to one serve, so you have to vary between backspin and no-spin.

So consider taking a 1-2-3 approach to serving: mentally prepare yourself, visualize the serve, and prepare for the follow-up.

DECEPTION

August 25, 2014 – Semi-Circular Motion on Serves

One of the most basic and yet misunderstood techniques at the intermediate level is the semi-circular motion used in serves for variation and deception. For beginners and intermediate players, the key is getting lots of spin, such as backspin, backspin-sidespin, sidespin, sidespin-topspin, and topspin.

While learning to do these spins there's little attempt to disguise the spin – the racket moves in one direction, the direction of the spin. But once you can do that it's time to learn to use semi-circular spin to disguise the spin. For example, for a forehand pendulum serve (with racket tip pointing down), you would start with the racket moving down, then down and sideways, then sideways, then sideways and up, and then up, like a pendulum. If I were to show you this motion and ask what spin it is, it's a trick question as you can't answer without knowing where in the serving motion contact was made.

Here's a video (7:24) showing this type of semi-circular motion serve by top players in slow motion:

www.youtube.com/watch?v=c9ZkNS-cz-I

Note that it's almost impossible to really study a top player's serve except in slow motion – at full speed everything happens too fast to see what they are really doing. In the videos one thing to look for is the amount of motion the racket does in directions different from the direction it goes at contact. Often the actual contact happens so quickly that even in slow motion it's difficult to pick up as the racket is rapidly changing direction at that point to confuse the opponent. The direction the racket is moving at contact is usually only for a split second, while the rest of the service motion exaggerates the racket moving in other directions. (Also note how after contact the racket often goes off in a different direction, sometimes away from the semi-circular motion, as an additional attempt to disguise the spin and confuse the opponent.)

At the higher levels, at full speed, the serves often don't look like semi-circular motions because the motion is done so quickly with a much shorter motion. But in slow motion you can see the racket go through this circular motion. It's not always a complete semicircle as parts of the motion are shortened for disguise.

This is one of the three important ways of disguising the spin on your serve. The other two are sheer amount of spin (making it hard to precisely read it), and spin/no-spin combinations.

December 23, 2016 – Racket Rotation Serve

Many players understand the importance of using a semi-circular rotation of the racket to create deceptively different spins. For example, with a forehand pendulum serve, the racket goes through a rotation that starts by going down, and then down and sideways, sideways, sideways and up, and then up. Depending where the contact is made you get different spins – backspin, sidespin-backspin, sidespin, sidespin-topspin, and topspin.

But you can get even more subtle than this. With the above motion, the axis of rotation at the start of the serve is the elbow, with the axis changing to the wrist just before contact. This means you get spin from both elbow and the wrist.

Now imagine snapping the wrist so that the tip is going *down*, but pulling up slightly with the elbow so that the bottom-left of the racket (near the handle, for a righty) is moving *up*, with the axis of rotation in the middle of the blade, i.e. the blade spins about its center. If contact is made near the tip, you get backspin. But if you contact it nearer the handle, you get sidespin or topspin! It won't be as much spin as with the standard forehand pendulum serve, but the amount of spin isn't nearly as important as fooling the opponent. In this example, the opponent will see the big downward swing of the racket tip, and will likely instinctively read the serve as backspin – and so you contact it near the bottom, with some combination of sidespin and topspin, and watch the opponent pop the ball up or put it off the end!

You can use this same principle with any semi-circular serving motion, though you should first master the standard version. Note that quickness of the motion is more important than the amount of spin – the goal is to trick them into thinking it's backspin, so exaggerate that motion. And then let loose with this new variation, and watch the looks of disbelief by opponents who were absolutely *certain* the racket was moving down at contact!

January 4, 2016 – Backhand Serve Deception with the Elbow

The key to deception on the backhand serve is the elbow. If you are serving backspin, you should vigorously contact the ball on the downswing, as much under the ball as possible, with a motion similar to chopping wood with a backhand motion. But the swing doesn't end there – you should follow through sideways and up by vigorously pulling up with your elbow. This forces the opponent to have to figure out if you contacted the ball on the down swing, or on the sideways or upward swing.

Similarly, when serving sidespin or side-topspin, you should start with this vigorous downward swing (chopping wood), as if serving backspin, but miss the ball, and instead contact it on the sideways or upward swing with that vigorous upward pull with your elbow. This time the elbow pull gives you spin instead of just being a fake motion. Again, the opponent has to figure out where you actually contacted the ball.

This principle actually applies to most serves, where your racket goes through some sort of semi-circular motion (often very short and abrupt, so opponent can't pick up the contact), where often are more vigorous on the part of the swing where you don't contact the ball. It's just a bit more obvious with the backhand, where much of the deception comes from the elbow. (But you still need a vigorous wrist motion for spin.) One advantage of serving backhand – you are facing your opponent, and so can see what he's doing as you serve. Some players can even change their serve, or at least service direction, in response to the receiver changing position at the last second.

SPECIFIC SERVES

September 19, 2016 – Five Serves That EVERYONE Should Master

Here are five serves that any serious player should have. Some you might use regularly; others you might use sparingly for a few free points each game. Many long-time players, even top ones, continually handicap themselves by not having the needed variations that would finish off an opponent – and often they don't even realize it, and so give away a few points every game that could be "freebies." Since there are three long serves (#1 below), and backspin/no-spin is two serves (#2 below), there are really *eight* serves everyone should have. But I like to group the deep serves together as "The Three Primary Long Serves" players will remember them when practicing serves, and when playing a match.

1. **The Three Primary Long Serves**, served from the backhand corner, often forehand pendulum serves.
    a. **Deep crosscourt breaking sidespin serve** that breaks away from the receiver (to the wide backhand if a righty serving to a righty). These serves throw off a receiver's timing and often leave them lunging for the ball. (This doesn't mean you should only do deep sidespin serves that break away from the receiver, but they are generally trickier to receive than ones that break into the receiver.) At the intermediate levels, a serve into the forehand that breaks away from the receiver can cause great difficulty, especially if not over-used. At the more advanced levels, that's not effective and so breaking serves are mostly into the wide backhand.
    b. **Fast no-spin at the elbow**. This serve is put in the net so

often it's a mystery every player doesn't develop this serve. It's the single most effective "trick" serve up to about 2200 level (which is pretty advanced) – almost a guaranteed point or two every game if done properly. Against players who cover the middle with their forehand the serve might be more effective into the wide backhand, or down-the-line if a righty serving to a lefty (or vice versa).

    c. **Fast down-the-line** (to a righty's forehand). Also effective **crosscourt** if served righty to lefty or vice versa. Many receivers try to cover more of the table with their forehand against deep serves, and so are vulnerable to sudden fast serves to the forehand. It also draws them out of position for the next shot. For righty vs. lefty or vice versa, there's a big angle into the forehand, so it can be even more effective unless the receiver moves over to cover that wide forehand – in which case they may be vulnerable to a fast down-the-line serve.

2. **Short backspin/no-spin to the middle.** By going to the middle, receivers have no extreme angles, and the server has less ground to cover on the follow-up. By mixing in backspin and no-spin, receivers often put the backspin in the net, and pop the no-spin up. It's important that these serves be very low to the net, and bounce twice on the far side if given the chance. If serving no-spin, use a vigorous motion as if serving with spin – you must sell it as if it's a backspin. If serving backspin, use less arm and more wrist so receiver will see less motion and think it's no-spin.

3. **Backhand-type sidespin from the middle, served short to forehand or long to backhand.** Many players are more comfortable receiving short serves with their backhands, and especially have trouble with backhand-type sidespin serves short to the forehand, which break away from them, and can be awkward to receive since to compensate for the sidespin they have to aim down the line, which is trickier with the forehand on a short ball. By serving from the middle of the table, it gives the server an angle into the short forehand that causes even more trouble, while putting the server in perfect position for the follow-up shot, which usually comes to the

forehand. Receivers often "cheat" and move in to cover this serve, even receiving it with their backhand – so be ready to use the same motion and suddenly serve long to the backhand, catching them off guard.

4. **Sidespin-topspin serve that looks like backspin**. This is the serve many top players use to serve weaker players off the table. Their racket tip is moving down at contact, so the serve looks like backspin, but the racket is rotating about its center, and so the bottom (near the handle, on the left for a righty) is moving sideways and up – and so the serve is side-top. Receivers often push it, and it pops up or goes off the end. Against stronger players, if you over use this serve they can attack it – so don't over use it, unless you are a counter-driving player. Use it sparingly, and it will give you free points.

5. **Sidespin that breaks both ways**. Some receivers are good against one type, not the other. Many players can only serve one type of sidespin effectively. Not only should you be able to do both, you should have motions where the receiver doesn't know which you are doing until you start your forward swing. The most common methods are forehand pendulum and reverse pendulum serves. But you can also do backhand regular and reverse serves and forehand tomahawk and reverse tomahawk serves.

November 9, 2015 – Sidespin Serves that Break Away Tend to Be More Effective

A backhand sidespin serve (or a reverse pendulum serve or tomahawk serve) tends to be more effective to an opponent's forehand, while a forehand pendulum serve tends to be more effective to the backhand. This is both because players often have to lunge after the ball as it breaks away, and because the racket angle needed to return these sidespins is less natural when done this way. Because the balls are breaking away from the table, it effectively increases the width of the table, forcing receivers to cover more ground. This doesn't mean only serving these serves to the side that they would break away from, only generally serving it more to that side. Each opponent is different, so try out each combination and see what happens.

Using this principle, you might want to develop the following four serves.

- Big breaking sidespin serve (from the backhand side) deep into the backhand that breaks away from the receiver, usually done with a forehand pendulum serve. This is very difficult for many receivers to handle as they often don't have as much range on the backhand as the forehand, and so end up reaching for the ball as it breaks away.
- Big breaking sidespin serve (from the forehand side) deep into the forehand that breaks away from the receiver, usually done with a forehand tomahawk serve. This serve is extremely effective through the intermediate level, but doesn't work very well at the higher levels, where they just loop it. But it's often a free point against many club-level players, who lunge for the ball as it breaks away and so lose control, usually lifting it off the end or side.
- Short sidespin serve (from the middle or forehand side) to the wide forehand that breaks away from the receiver, either bouncing twice on the table (given the chance) or going off to the side, usually inside the corner. It is usually done with a tomahawk, backhand, or reverse pendulum serve. Many players find this serve very awkward to receive as they have to reach over the table with their forehand, and then often end up lunging at the ball when it breaks away. Below the advanced level players almost always return this crosscourt, so you can almost camp out on that side and wait for the return.
- Short sidespin serve (from the backhand side) to the wide backhand that breaks away from the receiver, either bouncing twice on the table (given the chance) or going off to the side, usually inside the corner. This is usually done with a forehand pendulum serve. This often isn't as effective as one that breaks short into the forehand, but many players will have trouble with it, plus it takes out the extreme angle into the forehand, which is important for players who strongly favor the forehand.

So add these breaking sidespin serves to your repertoire, and give your opponents a case of the lungies!

September 1, 2014 – How to Execute a Fast Serve

These are rarely front-line serves as even intermediate players have little trouble attacking them if you use them too often. However, they are a great variation to spin serves, and if used a few times each game will often catch the opponent off guard. With experience, you'll get a feel for when and where to throw one of these fastballs at an opponent.

The keys to an effective fast serve are:

1. Speed
2. Depth
3. Placement
4. Spin (or lack of)
5. Consistency
6. Surprise

Let's look at how to execute the serve while doing all six.

- **Speed**. This is the whole point. The problem is most players don't understand how to maximize this, or chicken out under pressure. To serve fast, you must:
  1. Serve aggressively. You can't serve fast by patting the ball over the net.
  2. First bounce near your own end-line. You want to maximize the amount of table between bounces so the ball has a chance to drop. To do this you need to contact the ball far enough behind the end-line to allow this.
  3. Low contact point. Otherwise the ball will bounce higher and will take longer to drop and hit the other side, and so you won't be able to serve as fast.
- **Depth**. You want to serve as deep on the table as possible in order to jam the opponent. Just as important is that if the fast serve isn't going deep on the table then you aren't maximizing its speed. A fast serve should, by its very nature, go very deep or you aren't serving it very fast. There's a simple way to increase the depth of the serve – serve faster!
- **Placement**. All fast serves should go to one of three spots: wide forehand, wide backhand, or to the middle (the opponent's switchover point between forehand and backhand, usually the playing

elbow). Fast serves that go to the middle forehand or middle backhand are just feeding the opponent. Make him move to the corners or make a decision and move to cover the middle. To practice this, put targets on the far side of the table and see if you can consistently hit them.

- **Spin**. To maximize speed, put some topspin on the ball to pull it down. However, sometimes you want to vary this by serving with sidespin or a fast, dead (flat) serve, often at the middle. You can create topspin or sidespin by essentially slapping the ball with an upward (for topspin) or sideways (for sidespin) motion. You don't want to graze the ball too much with a fast serve as you won't get enough speed that way – that's how you create a spin serve. To serve a fast, dead serve, you need to contact the ball with a very slight downward motion, putting a very light backspin on the ball, sort of a downwards slap at contact, just as with topspin or sidespin. After two bounces on the table the ball will be dead.

- **Consistency**. It's pointless having a fast serve if you often miss it. You need to get a feel for both the proper contact with the ball and where to contact it (both the height and how far behind your end-line), and practice it until it's second nature. Then make sure to practice the serve before tournaments and big matches so you can execute the serve under pressure. As noted above under Placement, one way of practicing the serve is to put targets near the opponent's end-line and see if you can consistently hit them. You might also put a target on your own end-line and see if you hit that when you serve, to make sure that your first bounce is near your own end-line. Also, while some develop the serve by gradually building up the speed that they can serve fast, you might consider the opposite – serve as fast as you can, and gradually slow it down to the point where you can get it to hit the table. Then work at controlling that pace.

- **Surprise**. Your fast serve loses most of its effectiveness if the opponent sees it coming too soon. So set up as if you were serving your normal serves. Learn to do the fast serve from the same stance and starting with the same motion. The only difference might be that for a fast serve you might have to toss the ball back a little further so as to give yourself room to hit the ball so the first bounce is near your end-line, but if you do, that should be minimized. But your backswing should look the same whether you are serving fast or not. You don't want to telegraph to the opponent that the fast serve is coming.

NO-SPIN SERVES

October 19, 2015 – The Power of a Low, Short, No-Spin Serve

At the beginning level, players serve without spin. However, these serves are usually pop-ups that any intermediate (or advanced beginner) can easily attack. As players move up the ranks they learn to serve with spin. But eventually players come full circle and begin serving no-spin again. Yes, this is a shocker to many players, but sometimes nearly half of world-class serves are no spin serves. Why is this?

These no-spin serves aren't beginner-type no-spin serves. At the higher levels, there are two key differences: the serves are very low (whether no-spin or spin), and there's the *threat* of spin. Since the receiver isn't sure at first whether the serve has spin or not, he can't just assume no-spin, nor can he get into a rhythm against the no-spin since he's getting a variety of serves with spin.

But the key question is why no-spin serves are effective at the higher levels. It would seem that serving with spin is key, and that a no-spin serve wouldn't be much of a threat. But it doesn't work out that way. Here's why. (We're talking about short serves where, given the chance, the second bounce would be over the table. If the serve goes long, then spin or not, the receiver will likely loop it.)

If you serve short backspin, then it is rather easy for a top player to drop it short – the backspin makes this easy as it deadens the ball for you. With the incoming backspin reversing on contact with your racket, it's also easier for the receiver to put backspin on the ball, whether pushing short or long. On the other hand, if you serve no-spin, while it's easier to read the degree of spin (since no-spin always has the same degree of no-spin!), it's not as easy to drop it short. Nor is it as easy to put extra backspin on the ball, since there's no backspin on the incoming ball to reverse – you have to create all the backspin yourself.

If you serve short sidespin or topspin, it's easy to flip. The ball just jumps off the receiver's paddle, and comes out as a topspin, which makes it easy to control the flip. If you serve no-spin, the receiver doesn't have this jump, and has to create all the force of the shot himself, as well as any topspin to control the shot.

So the overall result is that it's harder to drop short or put extra backspin on a push against a no-spin serve short than against a backspin serve, and it's harder to flip aggressively against a no-spin serve than against a sidespin or topspin serve. (A key thing here is serving low – a no-spin serve that's slightly high gets attacked much more easily than a spin serve that's slightly high.)

There's still another advantage of a no-spin serve. While it's tricky trying to serve one spin while convincing the receiver it's another spin, it's probably easier to fake spin and serve no-spin. You simply contact the ball closer to the handle and put it over with a vigorous follow-through, faking spin. This is especially effective if you fake heavy backspin but serve no-spin – watch the opponent push this back and pop it up over and over! And then when you serve heavy backspin again, the opponent is often unsure of the spin, and so puts it right into the net.

So the lesson here is to learn to serve short with spin, and then mix in no-spin serves. You would be surprised how many top players consider the no-spin serve their "go to" serve when the score is close.

December 14, 2015 – Fast, Quick Motions Disguise a No-Spin Serve

Many players learn to put decent spin on their serves. However, when faced with disguising this spin, they have great difficulty. Why not develop a tricky no-spin serve, with a fast, quick serve contact? Change directions in the split second that the racket contacts the ball, where it is nearly motionless, or contact the ball near the handle of the blade (where the racket is moving slowest) so there will be little spin … but your opponent will be left making a snap decision on what's on the ball. Perhaps exaggerate one direction, often down, then snap the racket up at contact, leaving the receiver to figure where the contact was – and you have three options: on the down swing (backspin), as the racket is changing directions (no-spin), or on the sideways or upswing (light sidespin or topspin). A no-spin serve is just as effective as a spin serve if the opponent thinks there is spin on the ball!

December 7, 2015 – Use Simple No-Spin Serves in Doubles

In singles, you can serve to all parts of the table. This means you can usually force your opponent to receive from his weaker side, whether it's forehand or backhand. Not so in doubles! Now your opponent can choose his stronger side to receive. If you serve long, he'll probably attack it, usually by looping. If you serve short sidespin or topspin, he'll probably attack it as well with a flip. If you serve backspin, he can drop it short, push heavy, or flip it to a corner. What is a server to do?

Surprisingly, the answer is often a very shot, very low no-spin serve. At the world-class level, it's the most common serve in doubles, and often in singles. Why is this? A short no-spin serve is tricky to push – it's easy to pop up, and you can't put as much backspin on it, since you don't have a ball's spin to rebound off your racket – you have to create all your own spin. It's also not as easy to flip aggressively as a ball with spin since you can't use the spin of an incoming ball to help your flip. A topspin or sidespin ball rebounds out with topspin when struck properly. A backspin ball can be aggressively flipped, and the backspin continues, except now as topspin. (Often the receiver can put great topspin on this ball, especially with a backhand banana flip.) But a no-spin ball doesn't rebound out, and you can't use its non-existent spin. Plus, it's easy to keep a no-spin ball low. (A slightly high no-spin ball is easy to attack, so beware.) This doesn't mean you should serve all no-spin. But it can be the primary serve, with other serves used as variations, especially short, heavy backspin.

CHAPTER TWO: RECEIVE

June 15, 2015 – Good Receive is What Works

What is a good receive? It's whatever maximizes your chances of winning the point. End of story.

But let's elaborate. Many players fall into one of two bad habits when receiving: too passive or too aggressive. The ideal receiver can do both, depending on the situation. Plus, what might seem passive to some observers might, in the situation, actually be quite aggressive, such as a sudden quick and aggressive push or drop shot that catch the opponent off guard.

- **Too passive.** Usually this means players who push long against most backspin serves (even long ones), or make safe blocks or counters off topspin serves. Players like this develop great ball control, and if they have good defense (such as a good block), they can get away with this, to an extent. But these players are giving the server a predictable defensive return they can attack, and this becomes a lower and lower percentage as you improve and play better players. And yet, even at higher levels, a good push can be an effective return, as long as it really is a *good* push – quick and rather fast, deep, heavy or varied spin, low, and well angled, with the direction disguised or changed at the last second. But a long push receive is a lot more effective if the server doesn't know it's coming, so it's important for a good receiver to at least have the threat of something else – either an attack or (against a short serve) a short return.
- **Too aggressive.** Usually this means players who essentially attack every serve. While this is high percentage against deep serves (especially at higher levels), doing this over and over isn't usually the highest percentage receive against short serves. This is where variation becomes important – so learn to push long, short, and flip.

So what is the best receive? It's a combination of both of the above, but where each receive is chosen wisely so as to maximize your chances of winning the point. One could spend hours going over the possibilities, but all a player really needs to do is focus on one opponent at a time, and with a little experimentation and observation, figure out which receives will maximize your chances of winning the point.

If pushing over and over works, then that is the best receive; if attacking over and over works, then that is the best receive. Usually, but not always, the best is a mixture of the two, though that might take practice. Or you might get creative and use more advanced variations, such as sidespin pushes or blocks, changes of pace, and last-minute changes of directions.

There are at least two cases where you might not want to receive so as to maximize your chances of winning the point.

- **Mix things up**. You might receive in a way just to mix things up or give the server something to think about. For example, on a short serve to the forehand, if you don't have a good flip the better receive might be to push, but perhaps an aggressive flip will both make the server hesitant to serve there again, and make future pushes more effective as he guards against the flip.

- **Practicing for the future**. You may go for more advanced but lower-percentage (for now) receives so as to practice and develop the shot. For example, on that short serve to the forehand where pushing might be higher percentage you might want to flip so as to practice that flip, so that in the future, that might become a higher-percentage receive — and thereby making your receive that much better.

So find the right balance between passive and aggressive receives, while adding in variations and practicing for the future to find the ideal receive. And if you get it wrong, there's always the next serve.

February 10, 2014 – Never Give a Server What He's Looking For

Most players serve with a purpose. They are trying to get you to return their serve in a specific way so they can attack it. So . . . don't.

The classic case is the forehand looper who serves backspin to your backhand, anticipating a push to his backhand. He steps around and forehand loops. If he's got good footwork, he'll usually follow that shot with at least one more forehand loop unless you make a great return. So he's getting two forehand loops in a row, exactly what he wants.

Why not do a quick push to the wide forehand instead? If he's looking for a return to his backhand, you might catch him going the wrong way; many players have stronger forehand attacks from the backhand side (since the table isn't in the way); and if he does loop it, you can block to his backhand, and so he only gets one forehand attack. You've taken his game away from him and so have a much better chance of winning.

Or you could push the ball back short, and take away his loop altogether. Or you could attack the short serve. The key is to find something to do that he is not comfortable with. If he likes to follow his serve with a backhand loop if you push to his backhand, and a forehand loop if you push to his forehand, then perhaps do a quick push to the middle, rushing him as he tries to decide which side to attack with.

If your opponent likes to get into backhand exchanges, and so serves topspin, why give in to him? Learn to vary the return. Go to his forehand first, then quick to the backhand, so he has to both play his presumably less comfortable forehand, and then his backhand on the move. Or chop the serve back, which he doesn't want you to do, or he'd be serving backspin.

Suppose your opponent has tricky serves that you keep pushing and popping up, and he keeps smashing your returns. Why is your ball popping up? Because you're pushing against a ball that doesn't have backspin. (It could be topspin, sidespin, or no-spin.) He loves it when you push it since it sets up his smash. But since it's topspin, it should be easy (with practice) to return with a simple topspin shot. Shorten your stroke, control the shot back, and you'll take away what your opponent wants you to do. (Sounds easy, doesn't it?)

Corollary: Once you've established you are not going to give your opponent what he's looking for, a smart opponent will anticipate that, and expect you to do something different. That's when you cross him up with the return he was expecting before, but not now.

So next time you play, figure out what your opponent wants, and give him something else.

March 10, 2014 – Reading Service Spin

Returning serves effectively takes longer to learn to do than any other part of the game. This is due to the incredible variations in spin, speed, direction and depth available to servers. Worse, a good server disguises every aspect of the serve, especially the spin. We're going to focus on the most difficult part here – reading spin.

Ideally, a player should read the spin off the server's racket. No matter how many motions a server goes through, all a receiver has to do is read the direction of the racket at contact, and he will have read the type of spin. This is easier said than done.

The receiver also needs to read the amount of spin. Against a somewhat grippy inverted rubber, this is roughly done by a simple formula: racket speed – ball speed = ball spin. What this means is that a server's racket speed at contact will convert to ball speed and ball spin; if the racket moves fast, but the ball comes out slowly, then most of the energy has been converted to spin. (It's actually a bit more complicated than this. You get more spin if you accelerate into the ball rather than moving the racket at a constant speed, but it's close enough. Plus you have to take into consideration the grippiness of the rubber, as a non-grippy surface generate less spin.)

A server disguises spin in three major ways. First, his racket may go through a semi-circular motion, with contact at any point on the curve. This way, a server may give different spins with the exact same serve motion – the only difference is where in the serve motion contact is made. At the advanced levels, this semi-circular motion is so short and quick it's very hard to pick up.

Second, a server may disguise spin by mixing up spin and no-spin serves. (If a receiver thinks there is spin on the ball, and there isn't, it's the same as misreading a spin.) There are two ways the server may do this. A server may contact the ball near the handle of the racket, where the racket travels slower than the tip. Or he may fake a grazing motion, but just pat the ball with the racket straight on. In both cases, the server may use an exaggerated racket snap after contact.

Third, the server may put so much spin on the ball that it is simply difficult to read the amount of spin.

The only way to learn to return serves is to understand them, and to practice against them. So how do you read the spin?

As your opponent is serving, keep your eyes on his racket. (Against a high-toss serve, you may glance up to see when the ball will be coming down – but as it comes down, you should be watching the racket.) Ignore the direction the racket is moving until contact. Then, right at contact – SNAP! Take a flash "video" in your mind of the split second of contact. In this split-second video, you should be able to see the direction and speed the racket was going at contact. From this, you can judge the type of spin. From the racket speed, and the speed of the ball after contact, you can judge the amount of spin.

What happens if you absolutely cannot read the spin off the racket? Or if contact is hidden? If the contact is hidden (which isn't legal, though it often isn't enforced), you will have to read the spin mostly from the ball alone. The type of sidespin on the ball should be easy to read from the general racket motion – left to right or right to left. It's the reading of topspin vs. backspin that's tricky.

A ball with backspin tends to travel in a line, and slows down when it bounces on the table. A ball with topspin drops quickly, and jumps when it hits the table. A sidespin ball will curve sideways in the air, and jump sideways when it hits the table. If you let the ball come out to you and take the ball late, you will have more time to read this, and make the proper adjustments. However, reading from the ball alone will make your receive more tentative and late, and so less effective.

Eventually, reading spin will become more and more natural, and you won't even think about it so much. Then you can concentrate on what to do with the ball.

March 17, 2014 – Three Types of Receive Skills

Returning serve skills can be broken down into three specific skills. To be a great returner of serves you need all of them. The three are the ability to 1) read and react to the serve; 2) make consistent returns; and 3) make effective returns. Let's look at all three.

1. **Read and React to the Serve**.
   All the great shots in the world won't help you if you can't read and react to the serve. This means reading and reacting to what type of spin is on the ball; the direction; the depth; the speed;

even the height. You read the spin by watching the direction of the opponent's racket at contact with the ball, and by watching how the ball travels through the air and bounces on the table.

2. **Make Effective Returns**.

This means returning the serve in such a way that the server loses his advantage, and either get into a neutral rally or one where you have the advantage. For example, you may attack the serve by looping, driving, or flipping to put the server on the defensive. (Down side: it's easy to miss.) You may place the ball so the server is unable to follow with a strong shot. (Down side: it's not easy to receive accurately against a varied serve with lots of speed and/or spin.) You may push aggressively with heavy backspin to stop the server's attack. (Down side: Server may loop it, and turn your backspin into his own topspin.) You may push the ball back short so the server cannot loop. (Down side: it takes great ball control, and it's easy to pop the ball up, go into the net, or simply not push short enough.)

3. **Make Consistent Returns**.

It's not enough to make effective returns; you have to be consistent. Most top players will tell you that returning serves is all about ball control. They may attack the serve when they see the chance, but mostly they just want to neutralize things while being extremely consistent. This doesn't mean just pushing every serve back; it means using all of your receives to mess up the opponent, but doing so at a level where you rarely give away a free point.

Receive is often called everyone's weakness, but it doesn't have to be. Many players turn it into a strength. Why not you?

October 27, 2014 – Defensive or Offensive Returns of Short Serves

While this Tip is mostly about returning short serves, it also follows for those who aren't ready or able to loop against deep serves. At higher levels most players loop deep serves, and so only have to make a decision on what to do against shorter serves. At beginning and intermediate levels, however, players often do push against deep backspin serves. If they are going to do this, they should at least know how to approach this with their receive.

Many players look to push back most serves – and are caught off guard against topspin and sidespin serves, often popping them up or making a last-second change to a weak drive return. (You can chop down on these and sort of push them back, but it's often better to drive them back.) Others wait to see if the ball has backspin or not, then have to make a last-second choice between pushing (if the ball has backspin) or driving (if the ball doesn't have backspin). If the serve is no-spin, you can do either, but if you push you have to aim low.

If you want to reach the higher levels, it's often better to approach receive with the idea that you are going to attack all short serves – unless you make a last-second decision to push. In other words, rather than looking to push (and messing up against topspin/sidespin) or having to make a last-second decision between two choices (and so not being really ready for either), it's better to know what you are going to do and be decisive about it – and then change your mind at the last second if you see backspin. There are three primary reasons for this.

First, it's a lot easier to change your mind at the last second from attacking the serve to a simple push if you see backspin on the serve than it is to go from pushing to attacking the serve if you realize it isn't a backspin serve. It's easy to simply open your racket at the last second and push against a slow, incoming backspin ball, but it's tricky to close your racket at the last second and drive against a faster incoming topspin or sidespin ball.

Second, you can attack any short serve – even if it has backspin – and so if you decide in advance you are going to attack, you know you can do this. If you instead decide in advance to push the serve, you may get crossed up with a non-backspin serve. And if the ball does have backspin and you decide an attack is risky, it's easy to change your mind and switch to a push. There's nothing wrong with mostly pushing against backspin, though at higher levels you'd need to sometimes push them short or attack them.

And third, it gives you decisiveness. If you aren't sure whether you are going to attack or push, that can lead to indecisiveness, which leads to mistakes.

So look to be aggressive in your receives, with the option of switching to a push against backspin if you aren't confident in attacking it. You may still end up switching to a push most of the time against most backspin serves, but that's easy to do, and you'll be better at reacting to topspin/sidespin serves while learning to at least sometimes be aggressive against backspin serves. It's easier to be aggressive and switch to a push than it is to be defensive and switch to being aggressive, and it's always better to be decisive than to go in indecisively and having to make a last-second decision.

April 14, 2014 – Pushing Sidespin Serves Short

This tip is a bit technical mostly for higher-level players, but it is also for those who wish to understand the game at those higher levels. Thinking about spins and reacting to them in the way that we'll discuss here might give you a headache. You have been warned.

With practice, most players can learn to push short against a simple short backspin serve. However, it takes lots of practice to be able to do this in a match where you don't know in advance what type of serve you'll be getting. The problem with pushing short isn't so much against backspin serves, but against sidespin serves, which are often pushed back high and to the side. (Another problem is pushing short against no-spin serves that look like backspin, where you have to chop down on the ball, but that's a separate issue.) There's a somewhat simple trick for pushing these sidespin serves short.

Imagine a forehand pendulum serve (or another serve with this type spin) coming short to your backhand with mostly sidespin and perhaps some backspin. (We're assuming both players are righties; lefties can adjust.) If you try pushing short and don't adjust properly, the ball pops up and to your right. It's almost like pushing against a topspin. Now drop your racket tip some, and meet the ball a little on the bottom right side with a grazing motion, with a slightly downward motion. Instead of popping up to your right as it would when you push against sidespin, it'll return as if you were pushing a backspin because you are now meeting the spin head-on, as if pushing against a backspin. With this technique, you'll find it much easier to drop the ball short to the left, i.e. short to the opponent's forehand.

Now imagine a backhand serve (or another serve with this type spin) coming short to your backhand with mostly sidespin and perhaps some backspin. If you try pushing short and don't adjust properly, the ball pops up and to your left. Again, it's almost like pushing against a topspin. Now raise your racket tip some, and meet the ball a little on the bottom left side with a grazing motion, with a slightly downward motion. Instead of popping up to the left as it would when you push against sidespin, it'll go out as if you were pushing a backspin because you are again meeting the spin head-on, as if pushing against a backspin. With this technique, you'll find it much easier to drop the ball short to the right, i.e. short to the opponent's backhand.

With some adjustments, you can use this type of technique to drop the ball anywhere, but in general on the backhand side it's easier to drop a forehand pendulum serve type spin short to the forehand, and a backhand serve type spin to the backhand side. You can make the same adjustments with your forehand push, raising the racket tip some against forehand pendulum serve type spins, lowering it against backhand serve type spins. With practice, you'll find dropping the ball short against a short sidespin to be as easy as doing it against a short backspin. (Of course, pushing short against short backspin isn't "easy" unless you practice it to develop the light touch necessary – but it's a valuable tool to have against many players, so learn to do so.)

If you are having trouble visualizing all this, then imagine the opponent's forehand pendulum sidespin serve. Take a ball and actually rotate it with that type of spin as it comes toward you. Now imagine pushing it, and see how it would jump to the right (the opponent's backhand). Now drop the racket tip, and presto – you are meeting the spin head-on, like pushing backspin to backspin, and thereby getting much more control, just as you do when pushing against a backspin.

The same technique can also be used to push long, but is not always as effective there since for deep pushes you want to maximize the backspin. For this, you'd more likely just aim the opposite way as the sidespin, and chop down on the ball.

August 22, 2016 – Shorten Stroke When Receiving

Returning serves is all about ball control. In a rally, the incoming shot is usually more predictable than a serve, which normally has a much wider range of variation – topspin, sidespin, backspin, at all speeds and placements. To return serves, where the incoming ball is far less predictable, it helps to shorten the stroke to maximize control. This cuts down on power, but the shorter backswing gives you more control. (Just as with other strokes, the backswing and follow-through should still be about the same length.) The exception here is against a deep serve where you read the ball well, and so may use a normal loop stroke.

Watch the top players, especially against short serves. Do they rip the ball when receiving? Only occasionally, and when they do it's because of their extremely high level of play, or because the opponent made an error with their serve (a slightly long or slightly high short serve, or a "surprise" deep serve that doesn't catch the receiver off guard). Whether they are pushing (short or long) or flipping, it's all about consistency, control, variation, and deception. And for that, they shorten their swing and gain in all four categories.

December 26, 2016 – Last-Second Changes of Direction on Receive

Players learn to react to an opponent's motion as soon as they are committed. But some players commit early, others late. You can often see where an intermediate player is hitting his shot before he even starts his forward swing, while you normally can't tell against an advanced player until after he's started his forward swing.

Try adding last-second changes of direction to your game, especially when receiving. While it's valuable at all times, it is when receiving that you'll get the most bang for your buck by changing the direction at the last second. For example, if you are pushing aim to the backhand, and then, at the last second, as the server is reacting to it already, change and quick push to the forehand. Or do the reverse, aim to the forehand, and as he reacts to that, go quick to the backhand. You'll be surprised at how often you can mess up the server in this way. At first he'll likely get caught going the wrong way. Even when he adjusts, he'll be rushed as he'll have to wait longer to see where you are going.

You can do the same against sidespin-topspin serves, aiming one way, then going the other. It's one of the best ways to force an opponent to use his weaker side. Just aim to his strong side, then go to the weak side!

June 27, 2016 – Inside-Out Forehand Floppy Wrist Flip

When an opponent serves short to the forehand, many players reach in and return it with a nearly stiff wrist, and invariably go crosscourt with a forehand flip. Most players do this "Asian style," i.e. using the forearm to power the shot. This gives consistence and power, but less deception than the "European style" wrist flip. (The "Asian style" and "European style" monikers are from decades ago; these days many Europeans do it "Asian style" and vice versa, and many can do both ways.) To do this, approach the ball like any other flip. But at the last second, bring the wrist back, and brush the ball more on the inside (i.e. the back-left side of the ball, if you are right-handed). This puts the ball down the line, while your opponent has probably already moved to cover the opposite corner. The wrist must be very loose to do this shot. Advanced players can even sidespin the ball back with a right-to-left motion (for right-handers). Now, the next time you're at the club, you too can tell others that you now have the inside-out forehand floppy wrist flip. (Say that fast ten times. Another table tennis joy!)

January 18, 2016 – On Short Serves to the Forehand, Fake to the Forehand, Then Go Down the Line

Some players have difficulty with serves that go short to their forehand – it's awkward for them to reach over the table for those serves. However, there's a tradeoff – you get an angle into the server's wide forehand. This means that 1) you have more table (its 10.3 feet corner to corner crosscourt, vs. 9 feet down the line), 2) your opponent has more ground to cover on that wide forehand, and 3) you can move your opponent out of position by going to his wide forehand.

However, there's another option – fake crosscourt, but put the ball down the line. Often you don't even need to do this aggressively – just push or gently flip it down the line. What happens is that your opponent, knowing he has the wide forehand angle to cover, and also knowing that most players don't take the ball down the line as often, moves to cover that wide forehand angle. This leaves him open down the line – which is where you place the ball. Surprisingly, if you flip, it's sometimes better to do this shot softly, so your opponent can't use your own speed to rebound your ball back, making up for his being out of position and unable to make a strong shot on his own. A soft down-the-line flip will often completely disarm the server. (If you push, a somewhat fast and quick off the bounce one is highly effective.)

But key to this is to fake going crosscourt. It's only at the last second that you should tip your racket tip back from the forearm or wrist, aiming it to the right (for a righty), and take it down the line. Your opponent will be out of position, possibly over-anticipating a shot to his forehand, and will likely have to move back to his backhand, where he'll play a backhand shot instead of his likely stronger forehand.

For lefties vs. righties, there's a similar dynamic – fake down the line, then go crosscourt into the backhand. It's just as effective. In both cases, you've completely taken his serve advantage away, and forced your opponent to play a moving backhand. What more can you ask?

August 24, 2015 – Vary Your Receive – Exhibit A: Receiving a Short Backspin Serve to the Forehand

Many players have only a few receives off any given serve. This means they may be comfortable against those serves, but they aren't really doing anything to "mess up the server." How do you mess up the server? There are three ways.

- You can attack the serve. But that means going for relatively high-risk shots, and the advantage of the attack is often offset by the misses. Plus, if you attack every serve, you become predictable, and so the server is ready for it.
- You can neutralize the serve and get into a neutral rally. There are many ways of doing this, such as a short push, a well-executed deep push, or a well-placed medium attack. These are great options, but also become predictable.
- You can vary your receive so the server has no idea what you are going to do next.

This last one is the hardest for most players to execute as it means having numerous ways of returning any given serve. In many cases you only need a few options. But there are many times where having more options will pay off – plus, if you have many options, you are more likely to have the specific options that the server will have trouble with.

41

I'm going to go over an exercise I often demonstrate in clinics. I get a volunteer to serve short backspin to my forehand. (We'll assume the volunteer is a righty.) I have him do this over and over, and each time I give a different receive. On the next page is a list of some of the possibilities – and yet many players rely almost exclusively on one or two of these. You don't need to do all of these, but you should be able to do nearly all of them, and then pick and choose which ones are the most effective options against a given opponent – and then "cycle" through some of these options so the server never knows what's coming next. The list is just for receiving short backspin serves to the forehand; you should work out on your own the options on other serves. In general, you should look to have more options against short serves, and be more aggressive against long serves.

After going through the list, are you starting to see the possibilities? You don't need to learn all of these; pick the ones you like, and practice them until they are weapons in your arsenal, ready to pull out as needed to "mess up the server."

Possible Returns Against a Short Backspin Serve to the Forehand

1. Quick push to forehand.
2. Quick push to middle (opponent's elbow – when you go there you want to be quick).
3. Quick push down line to backhand.
4. Aim to wide forehand then quick push to backhand.
5. Aim to wide backhand then quick push to forehand.
6. Extremely heavy push to wide forehand.
7. Extremely heavy push to wide backhand.
8. Aim to wide forehand then sidespin push to wide backhand (ball breaking to right).
9. Aim to wide backhand then sidespin push to wide forehand (ball breaking to left).
10. Aim to wide forehand then push short to backhand.
11. Aim to wide backhand then push short to backhand.
12. Aggressive topspin flip to wide forehand.
13. Aggressive topspin flip to middle (opponent's elbow).
14. Aggressive topspin flip down line to backhand.
15. Aim to wide forehand then flip to wide backhand.
16. Aim to wide forehand then flip to middle (opponent's elbow).
17. Aim to wide backhand then flip to wide forehand.
18. Aim to wide backhand then flip to middle (opponent's elbow).
19. Flat but quick flip to wide forehand.
20. Flat but quick flip to middle (opponent's elbow).
21. Flat but quick flip to backhand.
22. Fake a push but at the last second flip – this gives you about ten more possibilities.
23. Step to right and flip with backhand – and suddenly you have lots of new possibilities as you can aim one way, go another, and go after the backhand, middle, or forehand.
24. When pushing, vary the contact point to throw off opponent's timing, sometimes taking the ball quick off the bounce, sometimes at the top of the bounce, and other times taking it later, which surprisingly throws many opponents off.
25. No-spin pushes!

CHAPTER THREE: STROKES

GENERAL

April 4, 2016 – Remember the Feel of the Good Shots

This one is short and sweet. From now on, whenever you hit a really good shot, *REMEMBER* the feel of that shot – the positioning, stroke, and contact. Then repeat. When you make a poor shot, put the feel of that one out of your mind like it never happened and remember the feel of the good ones. The *only* time to think about a poor shot is if you absolutely cannot figure out how to make it a good one, and so have to analyze it. That is all.

January 6, 2014 – Three Parts to a Swing

Backswing, forward swing . . . backswing, forward swing . . . backswing, forward swing . . . when hitting forehand to forehand or backhand to backhand, how many of you get into this pattern, whether hitting or looping? The problem is you are doing something you should never do in a match, so why would you want to practice it? There are *three* parts to a swing: Backswing, forward swing, and the often forgotten return to ready position. A player would almost never go directly from his follow through to backswinging.

Beginners and even relatively advanced players often warm up and practice as if there were only two parts to the swing, and it often costs them when it becomes habit. Often in real rallies they are set only for forehand or backhand, not both, because of this lack of return to ready position. If they don't do it in practice, why would they do it in a match? In reality, these players do tend to sort of return to ready after each shot, but either more slowly or not all the way, and so they often aren't ready for the next shot. For example, they'll hit or loop a backhand, and automatically bring their racket back after the follow through as if they were going to play another backhand, when of course they might be playing a forehand. And vice versa for forehands.

Instead, make a practice of returning to ready after each shot when practicing. On both forehands and backhands, this basically means the racket goes through a triangle, starting from the ready position: Backswing (bring racket back); forward swing (bring racket forward and up), and return to ready position (racket drops down and back to where it started, ready for the next shot). Usually these are essentially continuous, so there might not be any stop at the ready position; you go straight through the triangle, with the move to the ready position essentially the first half of the backswing, though it could continue into a backswing for either forehand or backhand. So drop the linear strokes and learn the triangle!

June 23, 2014 – Get the Backswing Right

I've written about the importance of Grip and Stance, and how getting these wrong is the root problem with most bad technique. If you have a good grip and stance, then all you really need to do is focus on a good backswing. If you have these three right, then like a bow and arrow that's been pulled back, the most natural forward swing is going to be good technique. (For this article, we're focusing on topspin shots, but the same principles apply to backspin shots.)

So how do you make sure you have a proper backswing? Ideally, work with a coach. But you can analyze yours, piece by piece. First, is it too short or too long? You generally want the same backswing each time. By doing this you get a repeating stroke that feels natural to the point where any swing that's too long or too short will feel wrong – a helpful self-correcting tool. If the swing is too long, it'll take too long (and so can't use it in a fast rally) and be too cumbersome (and so hard to control). If it's too short you won't have time to generate force, and so your stroke will either have little power or be too jerky to control.

Second, do you backswing to the right height? For flatter shots, backswing mostly back and slightly below the ball. For more topspinny shots, backswing lower. A backswing to the wrong height leads to all sorts of problems as you subconsciously try to adjust.

Third, do you backswing with the right racket angle? You don't want major changes in your racket angle once you start your forward stroke, so you need to get the angle right at the end of your backswing. For flatter shots, the racket should be mostly straight up and down, perhaps slightly closed. (Against backspin it might be slightly open.) For topspinny shots, the racket needs to be more closed. (Against backspin, it's more straight up and down, though when looping with power you should close your racket some even against backspin.) Many players backswing with the racket too open, and adjust by closing the racket during the forward swing, leading to a loss of control.

Once you have these three components of your backswing set, you can just let the shot go like an arrow. Your body's the bow, your arm is the string, and the ball is the arrow that's going to hit a bulls-eye to wherever you aimed it.

December 8, 2014 – Keep Your Strokes Simple

One of the secrets of coaching is that most of it isn't teaching someone what to do; it's teaching them what *not* to do. There's a reason top players make it look so easy – their strokes *are* easy, because they are simple and relatively short. There's no wasted motion, and very few actual components to each stroke – and each part of the stroke naturally leads to the next. A good stroke is a symphony of simplicity.

The best strokes are basically the most efficient ways of getting the racket to go from Point A to Point B while creating maximum power. Roughly speaking, correct grip and foot positioning are each one-fourth of the battle. Learning where Point A is – where the racket should backswing to, and the rest of the body's backswing motion – is another one-fourth of the battle. Then letting the shot go naturally and with proper contact is the final one-fourth. If you get the grip, foot positioning, and backswing correct, the rest is natural, though it is often amazing how many weird (and technically poor) incarnations of the stroke players can come up with. Most of these involve flopping the wrist or elbow, or holding back on part of the swing, such as stopping the body rotation so that you stroke mostly with arm, or swinging only with the upper body. Once you have this perfect (or near-perfect) stroke, then it's just a matter of developing the timing to turn it into a weapon of pong destruction.

Done properly, a good stroke is a thing of beauty that channels great power with minimal effort and maximum efficiency. It's the cartographical equivalent of driving from Point A to Point B. A coach's primary job is to get you buckled in properly for this journey (grip and foot positioning), get the backswing right (get you to Point A), and then set you on your way to Point B with no detours, and nothing but constant acceleration through the halfway point (contact) and continuing to Point B.

November 16, 2015 – Loose Grip Leads to Better Shots

Many players grip the racket too tightly. Many think this gives them added stability. Actually, all it does is tighten the muscles up by matching opposing muscles against each other rather than have them work together. It means that instead of smoothly executing a shot like the pros do, some of your muscles are trying to do the shot right while others are pressing back, making your shot ragged and erratic.

It also leads to injuries as muscles are forced to battle against each other while simultaneously executing table tennis shots. Players with tight grips leave the playing hall with exhausted muscles; players with loose grips leave with relaxed, loose muscles.

Here's a test. Imagine someone sneaking up behind you and grabbing your racket from your hand. It should come right out. If it doesn't, you're holding it too tightly. Conversely, it shouldn't be so loose as to wobble about in your hand, but that's rarely a problem.

September 15, 2014 – Should You Watch the Ball All the Way Into the Racket?

This is a common question. It really depends on the incoming shot. There's a general rule – if the ball is moving toward you slowly, watch it all the way into the racket. If it's moving toward you fast, you only need watch it to the point where you can no longer react to it.

Against slow balls, you should see contact. This includes serving, pushing, flipping a short ball, blocking against a slow loop, or smashing or looping against a push or other softly hit ball. (Of course, on some backhand shots actual contact is hidden by the racket.) It's also more important to see contact on more finely hit balls where you spin the ball by grazing it. You don't need to see contact as much on flatter shots, such as smashes, counter-hits, or blocks.

If the ball is coming at you fast, there's no point in watching it all the way into the racket since you can't react to it at the end anyway. So you only need to watch it until it is perhaps a few feet in front of you, depending on the speed of the ball. Against a medium-fast ball, you might watch it almost until contact.

Some players do appear to watch the ball all the way into the racket. This is probably just habit – rather than stop moving their head as they follow the ball toward their racket they simply get in the habit of following the ball all the way to contact. That's fine for some, and perhaps it helps with their timing. But there's no real need to watch the ball right until contact except against a slow-moving ball. One advantage of not watching the ball until contact is that you can look up more quickly and see what your opponent is doing, and so begin to prepare for your next shot more quickly. Some players even fool their opponent by sometimes looking up early in their stroke toward one spot on the table and then hitting it to another.

Here's a picture of Jan-Ove Waldner (considered by many the greatest player of all time) hitting a forehand where at contact he's already looking toward his opponent or where his ball is going: www.donic.com.tw/image-teams.files/Waldner_2004.jpg

POWER

September 22, 2014 – Power in Table Tennis

Some players can blast the ball a zillion miles per hour with hyperbolic spin while seemingly barely trying, while others grunt and grimace and can't break a soap bubble. So where does power in table tennis come from? Power comes primarily from eight factors. They are:

1. **Equipment**. Offensive rackets and sponges add to whatever power you put on the ball.
2. **Strength**. It makes a difference, though not as much as some would seem.

3. **Muscle Elasticity**. This is probably more important than sheer strength. It's a primary reason why older players, even if they weight train, lose power as their muscles lose their elasticity. Elastic muscles are like slingshots.

4. **Body Mass and Type**. If you rotate your body into the shot, you put your mass into the shot, and more mass means more power. You also might get more power potential from longer arms, the type of muscle (fast-twitch vs. slow-twitch), and even the way the muscles are connected.

5. **Type of Contact**. If you graze the ball too finely you lose the power potential from the sponge as well as speed. If you sink it directly into the sponge you gain speed from hitting directly into the wood, but lose power that might be generated by the sponge if you contact at more of an angle.

6. **Proper Technique**. This maximizes power generation as well as your ability to control it.

7. **Timing of Muscle Contractions**. Each muscle gets the next one started, and if it's not timed properly, you lose power.

8. **Timing of Contact**. If contact is not done at the point of maximum power, you lose power.

Let's elaborate on the last two – the timing issues. There are two types of timing when stroking the ball, and both lead to power. (Proper technique technically would include the two timing issues below, but I'm separating them here – but without good technique your power potential is severely limited.)

Timing of Muscle Contractions. Each muscle gets the next one started. The proper order for a forehand stroke is legs, hips, waist, shoulder rotation, shoulder, elbow, and wrist. (Wrist is optional on some shots.) If one contracts a muscle too soon or too late you lose power. If you contract any muscle too hard it becomes nearly impossible to control or to time them all together, so you only contract at whatever percent you can consistently and smoothly control – perhaps 70%, perhaps more on easy high balls.

Timing of Contact. Contact should take place when the racket approaches maximum speed. Technically, you shouldn't contact the ball when the racket is at maximum speed; you want to accelerate through contact, meaning the racket actually speeds up as you contact the ball, and so is *slightly* faster the split second after contact. (This might be where physicists can chime in, but from a coaching point of view, this is a key issue – far too many players lose power because they stop accelerating before contact, thereby dissipating some of their power. Or is this an illusion, and you get maximum power by reaching maximum velocity right at contact, meaning zero acceleration at that point?)

So how can you increase your power? All of the items above are factors, though I don't recommend gaining weight (other than muscle mass) to increase power. (I'm not sure how much of a factor that really is, but it's greatly offset by the loss of mobility.) Physical training can help with strength and muscle elasticity. But most of power potential comes from items 5-8 above. A coach can greatly help you with these. When I watch players who have trouble generating power – which is most players – I find that the most common problems are those that a coach can solve – the technique and timing issues. Grunting and grimacing are just indications that the player is having technique and timing problems that keep him from getting that easy power that comes so easily to some players.

September 7, 2014 – Easy Power

What is "easy power"? It is the ability, through proper technique, to generate great force in your shots, whether it's looping or smashing. Given a high ball and enough time, most players beyond the beginning stage can hit the ball pretty hard. But often they strain to do so, which costs them both power and consistency. Players with good technique can do the same without straining, and end up with more power and consistency. Most of us have seen such players, who seem able to generate point-ending power (both speed and spin) with ease while others strain to do so. What is their secret?

It's all about timing and using the whole body. Most players, when hitting or looping hard, strain to add power, and the result is they get nearly 100% force from only a few muscles, from the upper body and arms. They are losing the power from the lower body, from the legs and waist. (Some may use waist, but without the legs you can't really use the waist muscles effectively.)

Watch videos of top players as they rip forehands, and see how they almost rock into the ball as they rotate into the ball, smoothly putting their entire body into the shot. They aren't even using 100% power from any of these muscles, because to do so would mean to basically jerk one muscle at full power, and so you only get power from that one muscle – and you can't really control a muscle that contracts at 100%. Instead, use all the muscles, but at perhaps 70%. This allows you to use them all in smooth progression, from legs to arm. When you can do this, you too will have "easy power" – and both your power and consistency will shoot up.

Below are two videos of Wang Liqin (three-time world men's singles champion) that illustrate this. He is considered by many to have had the best forehand loop of all time. In the first he is looping in a drill (45 sec, including slow motion), where you can see how he rotates all of his body into the shot, starting with the legs and moving up to the arm. In the second he's ripping a winner (9sec, also slow motion replay).

Video 1: www.youtube.com/watch?v=_ppw7NT9g1w
(or Google "The Shot That Owned a Decade").
Video 2: www.youtube.com/watch?v=5KmGN6BRLFw
(or Google "Wang Liqin crazy spin").

January 13, 2014 – Maximum Power and Control

How do you get maximum power on your shots? Many players at the beginning/intermediate levels might say "swing hard!" But that's the worst thing you can do. Until your muscles are trained properly, swinging hard means spastically using a few muscles but not all of them. It also means putting less weight into the shot. Both cases result in either wimpy shots that any well-trained kid would laugh at, or sometimes powerful shots with no control.

Watch a baseball pitcher with a good fastball. (You can find many at Youtube.com) Many of them can break 100mph, and nearly all are in the 90s. Watch these flamethrowers; are they swinging hard, or are they swinging *smart*? I think you can see the answer; the most powerful throwers don't seem to put full effort into their pitch; in fact, their throws seem effortless. And they're able to hit a rather small target from over 60 feet away.

Now watch the top table tennis players, and you'll see the same. The shots of the most powerful players often seem effortless. Meanwhile, watch some intermediate players as they swing as hard as they can, usually with less power and always with less consistency. Many spastically use one or two muscles at full power while losing the power of everything else, including their body weight rotating into the shot. Their shots spray all over the court as you cannot control a muscle spastically contracting at full power.

A key here is that these baseball pitchers and table tennis players not only have power, but they have control. How do they do it? The secret is they use their full bodies in a fluid motion that rotates everything smoothly into the shot, leading to power and control. It starts from the legs, then the hips, then the waist, then the shoulders, then the arm, and finally the wrist, which effortlessly snaps into the ball like the tip of a whip. All these muscles are engaged as the player accelerates into the shot, creating the seemingly effortless power of a pitcher or top table tennis player.

It is the addition of all these smooth muscle contractions and rotations, in the proper sequence (from bottom to top, and roughly from big muscles to small) that gives great power and control. So here's a good rule: never swing at 100%. Swing smoothly, using the full body, at perhaps 70-80% full power, and watch the power and control shoot way up.

February 22, 2016 – Three Tips to Increase Forehand Looping Power

If you are the type of player who has trouble generating power when looping, try out these three tips, and you'll be surprised at the improvement.

First, keep your legs farther apart, i.e. a wider stance. This makes it easier to transfer weight into the shot, meaning more power. Watch videos of the top players and you'll see how they all keep a pretty wide stance.

Second, contact the ball more from your side. Many players contact the ball too much in front of their bodies, and so they get power mostly from their arms. By contacting more to the side, you get more natural body rotation into the shot, meaning more power.

Third, tilt your wrist slightly back. This will naturally give you more wrist in the shot – and you'll likely use more forearm as well as you use it naturally to snap the wrist into the shot.

By following these three tips, you'll get more power without really trying since none of these involve trying to "muscle" the ball – it's all about good habits that allow you to maximize your natural power.

FOREHAND

November 7, 2016 – Three Ways to Play the Forehand

Even if you are a backhand-oriented player, you still need to play forehands. Many have difficulty with this because they stand in a backhand stance, and have difficulty switching to a forehand stance. Even some forehand players, once they play a backhand, go into a backhand stance, and have trouble with their forehand after that. So how do you go from playing a backhand to a forehand? There are three basic ways.

- **Pull Back Leg Back for Forehands**. (When we say back leg, we mean the right leg for righties, the left for lefties.) A player in a backhand stance often has his legs either parallel or the back leg actually in front (i.e. a righty has his right leg in front). To play a forehand in this manner, he needs to pull the leg back quickly, rotating the body around, to get into a forehand stance. This is the most standard way, and the choice for most players. However, many backhand-oriented players, especially those who do not train regularly, have great difficulty with this. It's all a matter of training to make it a habit.
- **Play Forehands with a Neutral Stance**. This was considered a no-no in the past, but in the modern game, which is faster and more two-winged, most top players learn to play with their feet mostly parallel to the table. This gives them a strong backhand. When playing forehand, if rushed or close to the table, rather than pull the back leg back, they simply rotate the body at the hips and waist. This takes a lot of training, including physical training. But once mastered, it allows players to play a strong two-winged attack without backing up.

- **Play Backhands with a Forehand Stance.** This was very common in the past, but less common these days as backhand techniques have advanced and more and more players develop their backhands into strong weapons. If you play a mostly blocking or consistent backhand, then you can do this with a forehand stance, with right leg back (for righties). This allows you to play quick backhands and make a very quick transition to forehand play since you are already in a forehand stance. (Note – this is how I generally play my backhand.)

November 14, 2016 – How to Develop a Quicker Forehand

Many players have sluggish forehands. Some are forced to back up, while others stay at the table but make awkward shots. How can you develop a quicker, more effective forehand?

First, it's all about technique and footwork. If you have poor forehand technique, then you will likely struggle with your forehand shots, period. So work on the technique. This might mean working with a coach, but isn't it worth doing that a few times rather than face a lifetime of frustration?

Once your technique is relatively solid, you can go about making it quicker, allowing you to make those quicker, more effective shots you see top players do so smoothly. How do you go about doing this?

Practice. But not just practice – just as with any other aspect of your game you want to develop, it must be proper practice. In this case I have three drills to recommend for developing that quicker forehand. I swore by these three when I was developing, and they helped me develop a quick forehand, both hitting and looping.

1. Partner blocks or strokes side to side as you alternate forehands and backhands. Your focus is to move side to side smoothly, and play the forehand a little quicker than usual. The reason is if you can do it quickly here, it'll transfer into game situations. I used to drill with a lefty on this drill, allowing me to play into their backhand – my forehand crosscourt, looping quick off the bounce, my backhand down the line. With a righty, you can play into their forehand or backhand.

2. Partner blocks or strokes side to side randomly, you react with forehand or backhand, trying to play the shots a little quicker off the bounce than usual. Don't anticipate in this drill; just react. Watch your partner's racket, and you should be able to see where he's going the instant he starts his forward swing, allowing you to jump on each ball, which should become a habit. This drill develops quicker reactions and shots in game situations, as well as a quick return to ready position after each shot.

3. Hit backhand to backhand with your partner, aggressively, where he randomly picks out one to suddenly go to your forehand, then play out the point. Now you are not only practicing a quick return to ready position after each shot – absolutely necessary in this drill or you'll get clobbered – but a quick move to cover the forehand when the ball goes there. From drill #2 above you should be reacting a little quicker to your partner's shots, so you should be able to cut off those shots to the forehand more quickly than before. As in drill #2, don't anticipate; just react, and jump on each ball as you see where it's going to go, just as you want to do in a match situation.

October 12, 2015 – Back Foot Position on Forehand

One of the technique changes in the sport over the past few decades has been the gradual evolution of the back foot placement on the forehand from the standard position, with the right foot back (for a righty), to the feet often being parallel. This is not advisable for beginners, not until they have made the proper forehand rotation a habit. But as you learn to play faster and faster, and closer to the table, there's less time to move the foot back. This means some loss of power, but an increase in quickness – and that payoff is enough for most world-class players.

This only applies to shots taken near the table in a fast rally, where top players often take the ball at the top of the bounce or even on the rise. By keeping the feet parallel, they can execute these shots more quickly. (This is true for both hitting and looping, but these days loopers with tensor-like sponges dominate.) It's a riskier shot, taking good timing, but is often unreturnable, with the opponent often still recovering from the previous shot as yours whizzes past him.

There's an additional benefit. By keeping the feet parallel, you are forced to rotate backwards more at the hips and waist, which mostly makes up for loss of power from not having a foot back to push off from.

The question then is whether you should attempt this type of foot positioning on forehands. It depends on your level, quickness, fitness (in particular a supple waist), style of play, as well as your willingness to play riskier shots. Do you like living a little on the wild side, or playing it safe with the foot back?

Once you have reached an intermediate level, and can play forehands effectively, you can look to develop this shot. But it does take a supple waist to make up for that lack of the foot being back. If you train regularly and practice this shot properly, you'll develop that supple waist as well as the timing needed for the shot. It'll always be a somewhat risky shot, but the reward is both an often unreturnable shot, and the realization that you've just pulled off a genuine world-class shot.

May 23, 2016 – Contact Point on the Forehand

Many players lose power on their forehand because they contact the ball too much in front of the body. This means they aren't really rotating into the ball with maximum efficiency – instead, as they are about to contact the ball, they are using mostly arm, which is moving forward while the body lags behind.

Instead, try contacting the ball more to the side of the body, by your right leg (for righties). Imagine there's a rod going through the top of your head, and circle the rod, as Ma Long does in this 48-sec video (www.facebook.com/1besttt/videos/485926864944603). By doing this you'll naturally rotate into the shot, getting maximum power and efficiency. This is true for both looping and regular drives.

Note that the goal here isn't just to get lots of power; it also leads to better control since you'll be getting the same amount of power (speed and spin) but with less effort. The more effort you have to put into a shot, the less control, so develop efficient shots where you minimize effort while maximizing power.

Here are the forehand contact points for these players – or choose your favorite player and Google that player's name along with forehand loop pictures.

- www.larrytt.com/images/Ma-Long.jpg
- www.larrytt.com/images/Xu-Xin.jpg
- www.larrytt.com/images/Fan-Zhendong.jpg
- www.larrytt.com/images/Zhang-Jike.jpg
- www.larrytt.com/images/Dimitrij-Ovtcharov.jpg
- www.larrytt.com/images/Timo-Boll.jpg
- www.larrytt.com/images/Joo-Sehyuk.jpg
- www.larrytt.com/images/Liu-Shiwen.jpg
- www.larrytt.com/images/Ding-Ning.jpg
- www.larrytt.com/images/Zhu-Yuling.jpg

LOOPING

November 17, 2014 – Smooth Acceleration + Grazing Contact = Great Spin

The two most common mistakes players make in failing to create great spin are 1) a lack of smooth acceleration, and 2) grazing contact, which are the two pillars of creating spin, whether it be serving, pushing, chopping, or slow looping. (For faster looping, you sink the ball more into the sponge, but the smooth acceleration part holds for all looping.) I'm mostly writing for players using inverted sponge, but the same principles apply to most pips-out surfaces as well, as long as they have some grippiness.

When looping, players below the advanced level often try to get extra spin by "muscling" the ball, meaning they try to use nearly 100% of their muscle power as they go for maximum racket velocity. The actual result is they only use a few of their upper-body muscles (often mostly arm), and a loss of control. When they learn to slow down and use all their muscles (at perhaps 70%) and smoothly accelerate into the ball, that's when they get the acceleration needed for powerful loops with both spin and speed. That's why the most powerful loopers often make it look effortless.

When serving and pushing, beginning and intermediate players often use a short stroke and sort of jab at the ball. They are thinking that the velocity they get with this jabbing will create great spin. Actually, it just leads to a loss of control as you can't control the racket this way.

Plus, for physics reasons I won't get into (partially because I'm not a physicist), you get more spin if you smoothly accelerate into the ball, with the rubber literally slinging the ball out as it accelerates through contact. (When looping with both speed and spin, where you sink the ball more into the sponge, it should feel like you're almost holding the ball on your racket as it carries it through the shot, with an even greater slingshot effect.)

But on slow spin shots (serving, pushing, chopping, slow loops), you only get this tremendous spin if you graze the ball – the second problem many players have. Too often players sink the ball too much into the sponge instead of the fine grazing motion needed. To learn to graze the ball, just toss one up and graze it with your racket, making it spin. Generally do this with a pendulum serve motion, but contact the ball on the *left* side of the ball (for a righty), with the racket going mostly up and slightly left, so that the ball goes straight up. Catch it and repeat. It's important to spin the ball so it goes straight up, both so you can catch it and repeat, and so you can develop ball control. (If you can't control the direction the ball goes when you graze it with this exercise, how can you do it when actually serving?)

I recommend beginning players get a multi-colored ball or put markings on one so they can practice grazing and see the spin they are creating. This gives feedback on whether you are really spinning the ball or not and how much.

For more advanced players, I recommend they also do the ball spinning drill I wrote about above. It's a great way to really develop those grazing skills so you can both spin the heck out of the ball and control it. Advanced players should also experiment with smooth acceleration and grazing on their spin shots, and see how much they can make the ball spin.

When you can put great spin on the ball with your serve, apply the same principles to pushing and slow looping. (Also chopping if that is in your arsenal.) Don't be afraid to throw in some slow, spinny loops, even if you normally loop pretty hard. Slow, spinny loops are extremely effective at the beginning/intermediate level, but many forget or never realize how effective they are even at the advanced level if not overused. They not only are effective on their own as the opponent struggles to adjust to the slower speed and higher spin, but the contrast makes your other loops more effective.

November 2, 2015 – Distance from Table When Looping a Push

One of the common problems I see are players who stand too far from the table when looping against backspin. They'll stand well off the table, with their contact point in front of them. This means that to put their weight forward, they have to fall slightly backwards to compensate. It's either that or resorting to a rather soft loop, with mostly upward motion, and little speed.

Instead, learn to almost jam the table with your left leg (for righties) when looping backspin. This allows you to rotate properly into the shot, even with the same contact point as the players who back up, since you'll be contacting the ball to the side of your body instead of in front. But now, with body torque, you'll have tremendous power, and so able to loop at all speeds.

Having tremendous power does not mean you loop every ball with great speed. It means you effortlessly create power, and that power goes into both speed and spin. Go for about 50-50 on most shots, going for more speed against a weaker push or when you've really read it well.

Standing closer to the table also allows you loop backspin a bit quicker. Some players even take them on the rise, but for speed loops, it's best to take them at the top of the bounce; for more consistent loops with a higher spin to speed ratio, take them perhaps slightly on the drop.

While this article was written about looping backspin, it all applies to looping against topspin as well, except the positioning is a bit more complex, depending more on the incoming ball. But against a softer topspin ball, you'd also want to stay close to the table and generally loop it around the top of the bounce, or even on the rise.

Here are three examples from the final of the recent Men's World Cup. These players don't push long a lot, so in the first game there were only three long pushes where the other player forehand looped, twice by Ma Long, once by Fan Zhendong. Watch how close they are to the table in all three cases. Go to Youtube.com and search for "2015 Men's World Cup Highlights: MA Long vs FAN Zhendong (Final)." Then look for these three shots:

- **Ma Long** 1 (7 sec in)
- **Fan Zhendong** (59 sec in)
- **Ma Long 2** (93 sec in)

So remember – when you want to jam a loop down your opponent's throat, jam the table!

September 5, 2016 – Looping Slightly Long Balls

Many players have great difficulty looping slightly-long balls, especially with the forehand. These are usually serves or pushes that go only a little bit off the table. Most players push them back – and since the ball is relatively deep, they can't get a good angle nor can they rush the opponent with a quick push, and so their return is ineffective. The solution, of course, is to loop these balls. (And the nice thing here is that when you read these balls right, they are easy to loop very aggressively.) How do you learn to do that?

Here are three tips for learning to forehand loop against slightly-long balls. (Tips 2 and 3 apply to the backhand loop as well.)

1. You need to be very close to the table, with your head directly over the end-line. This allows you to look down on the ball, making it much easier to see if the ball is long, as well as easier to time it.

2. Realize that you can loop a ball even if it is actually slightly short, i.e. the second bounce would be on the end-line or even an inch or so inside. You simply stroke aggressively over the table with a slightly upward stroke. Once you realize this, you'll see that balls that seemed unloopable are actually very loopable. (You can go over the table even more with the backhand loop, by using more wrist. In fact, a backhand banana flip is essentially a loop done over the table.) Some worry that they'll hit their hand on the table, but if you are aware of where the table is, you just stroke slightly behind or above it. If you can contact a small, moving ball, how hard is it to avoid hitting a large stationary object? (In 40 years of play, I don't recall ever hitting my hand on the table while looping.)

3. *Practice!* How do you do this? Have someone feed you multiball backspin where the ball is only slightly long, or do it live where you serve and your partner pushes the ball back slightly long. You'll have to adjust to each shot as some will be longer, some shorter, including some too short to forehand loop. Get your head over the ball (see #1 above), recognize that you can loop balls that you didn't think you could before (#2 above), and loop

those that are loopable. At first, if you think the ball is unloopable, *let it go*. You'll be tempted to adjust and either push or flip, but letting it go is the only way to get true feedback. Watch it and ask yourself, "Could I have looped that ball?" Often the answer will be yes. Eventually, with practice, you'll be able to judge this, and then you can stop letting the ball go, and practice either looping the loopable ones, and pushing or flipping the shorter ones.

BLOCKING AND DEFENSE

December 29, 2014 – Brick-Wall Blocking Defense

Ever play one of those players who can seemingly block *everything* back? How do they do that? It's almost as if they are playing the video game Pong – they just don't miss. You can do the same thing. Here are three keys.

First, get your racket behind the ball. This may sound simple, but it's key. If you get the racket behind the ball, then all you have to do is have the right racket angle, and the ball goes back! But how do you get the racket behind the ball? That involves proper ready stance, a clear mind, and moving your feet.

A proper ready stance means you are equally ready to move either direction. This usually means the racket tip is pointing directly at the opponent's contact point. (Some players who contact the ball quicker on the backhand hold the racket slightly turned to the backhand, since they have less time to react on that side. If they do, they often compensate by having their feet in a slight forehand stance.)

A clear mind means you are ready to react to the ball rather than trying to anticipate. Just watch the opponent as he hits the ball and react. Don't think or guess; just react. The only time you anticipate is when you have popped the ball up so weakly that guessing where the ball is going the only way you can react to the next shot. However, if you can read where your opponent is going early in his stroke, that's not anticipation – that's reacting, and you should react. Never react so early as to let the opponent see this early enough that he can change directions.

Moving your feet means exactly that – step to the ball rather than just reach. Some do get away with mostly reaching, but that limits your range and hurts your control.

Second, good contact. This means blocking firmly against heavy topspin. If you just hold the racket out, the spin will take on your racket and shoot up. So put a bit of firmness into the shot. Learn to use the same contact every time so you can develop your timing and precision – and then learn to change speeds.

Third, practice. Lots and lots of practice. There are plenty of players looking to work on their attack, so oblige them. The more you practice your blocking the more you'll become one of those players who seemingly block *everything* back.

May 9, 2016 – Move In to Cut Off the Angles with Quick Blocks

A common problem when blocking (both forehand and backhand) is to cover the wide angles by stepping (or worse, reaching) sideways, and letting the ball come to you. While you do, of course, have to move sideways to cover these shots, a key part is moving *in*, and catching the ball quick off the bounce. By moving both sideways and in, you can do the following:

- Catch the ball before it has a chance to move even wider, which would force you to cover even more court;
- Make a more aggressive block, which is easier to do when moving in than when moving sideways;
- Stay in position since you don't have to move as much sideways, so you will be more ready for the next shot;
- Rush the opponent by taking the ball earlier;
- Angle the opponent right back. And since you have the potential for this wide angle, if your opponent over-reacts to cover it, you can go the other way, forcing your opponent to cover a lot of ground.

How do you do all this? By stepping in and sideways with the near foot. On blocks to your left (the backhand for a righty), step sideways and in with your left foot. On blocks to the right, step in and sideways with the right foot. In both cases recover quickly by stepping back.

So when your opponent is attacking at wide angles, learn to cut off those angles by stepping in, and turn a potential weakness into a strength as you turn the tables on the opponent with your own aggressive, quick-angled blocks.

October 3, 2016 – Returning Smashes: Reacting and Racket Angles

How often have you given up on a ball that your opponent is about to smash or loop-kill? And how many times have you gotten your racket on the ball against an opponent's smash or hard-hit ball, only to put it off the end, further re-enforcing the futility of trying to win such points? It happens all the time. And it's a crime.

Some will no doubt argue they don't have the fast reflexes of a pro to return smashes. That's a myth. You have fast enough reflexes, just not the proper *reactions*. A pro doesn't see an incoming smash and react with incredible reflexes; he sees an opponent's forward swing coming toward the ball, and reacts well before contact to where he sees the ball must be going. It's that big head start he gets that makes him seem to have supernatural reflexes. He's both moving into position and setting up for his return before the opponent even hits the ball. How do you learn to do this? By observing opponents and trying to read where their shots will go from their forward swing. If you do this regularly, it becomes a natural habit, and you'll start reacting faster and faster. Most top players are barely aware of doing this since they've been doing it for so long, often since they were little kids, and so it's all subconscious reactions.

But once you've reacted to the ball, you still have to return it. Here's something you should live by when facing a smash or loop-kill: If you can get your racket on the ball, you should get it back. Unlike a loop, a smash doesn't have much spin, and so the racket angle needed for returning a smash is easy to anticipate. All you have to do is practice getting the right angle, and lo and behold, if you touch it, it'll go back. The same is actually true against a loop-kill as well – the racket angle needed to return one is almost the same for all, so once you get that angle, you can return them. (It's often the topspin jump off the table that gives many players fits against a strong loop.)

How do you practice all of this? That sort of answers itself; you practice it by having an opponent practice his smash (or loop-kill) while you block, counter, or fish. (No lobbing for this exercise.) At first have them go to one spot so you can practice getting the right racket angle until it's second nature. Then have them move the smash about, and you watch their swing and try to see where their smash is going. Keep your shots deep; if you put the ball high and short, you have little time to react and they'll have extreme angles. Soon you'll be returning these "put-aways" like a pro – at least some of the time.

May 5, 2014 – Returning Smashes and Loop Kills

Starting at the intermediate level players begin to realize that they can actually return put-away shots, whether it's by blocking, countering, fishing, lobbing, or chopping. There's no magically fast reflexes needed, just a little knowledge and technique. Here are some tips on how to put pressure on your opponent by returning their put-aways – and remember, they are often off balance and rushed if you return them, and will often miss the next shot.

1. **Depth**. Probably the most important part of returning a put-away shot takes place with your previous shot. If that shot landed short on the table, then you both have little time to react to the opponent's shot and you have more ground to cover since you've given the opponent a wide angle. So if you are going to make a weak shot that the opponent is going to try to put away, keep the weak shot deep on the table.

2. **Away from Table**. You need time to react to the opponent's put-away, so step away from the table to give yourself time. Even blockers may have to block from a step back.

3. **Ready Stance**. You need to be in a proper ready stance that allows you to quickly move in either direction. This means feet at least slightly wide, weight on balls of feet, knees bent, leaning forward slightly from the waist, racket in front of you pointing at the opponent.

4. **Watch and Study Your Opponent**. You can read the direction of a put-away shot before your opponent hits the ball. First, watch his shoulders. They usually line up in the direction of a forehand shot. Second, watch the direction of the forward swing, which should also tell you the direction. Third, be aware of the opponent's position. If he's way around his backhand corner but facing toward your backhand, it might be difficult for him to go down the line, and so he'll likely go crosscourt. And fourth, be aware of your opponent's habits. Many players will go the same way over and over, often crosscourt, so if necessary you can anticipate that direction.

5. **Step to Ball**. Amateurs react to a hard-hit ball by reaching; top players react by stepping, and reaching only when necessary. Many players believe they just don't have time to step to the ball, but that's because they have developed the habit of reaching instead of the habit of stepping. Learn both; you can cover more ground more quickly if you both step and reach.

6. **Placement**. The goal isn't just to return the put-away shot; the goal is to win the point. If you can return a put-away shot, you can also place it. So focus not only on getting the ball back but on placement and depth. Depth is a must or the opponent will just cream the ball again, and likely won't miss. Keep it deep, and he'll make more mistakes and you'll have a better chance of continuing the rally. If you move the ball side to side you are more likely to force a mistake.

7. **Practice**. Of course you can't return a put-away shot in a game if you don't practice it. Can you do anything at a relatively high level in a game without practicing it first? So find ways to practice returning put-aways. It'll not only make you better at returning these shots, it's fun!

8. **Confidence**. It's not enough to just go through the motions; you have to believe you can do it. If you are confident you can return a shot you won't hesitate to go for the return, and you'll have a much better chance of making the return. Just watch your opponent and the ball and let your subconscious react. With practice, it'll become easier than you'd think. Decide what your primary way of returning a put-away shot will be (blocking, countering, fishing, lobbing, or chopping) and become a master of that shot.

PUSHING

June 13, 2016 – The Difference Between a Drop Shot and a Short Push

Are these the same things? Almost. A drop shot typically is made as short as possible, and is usually used against a chopper caught off the table. The goal here is to keep the ball as short as possible so that the defender either can't get to it (an "ace"!), or is lunging to get it, and either can't make a good return or recover for the next shot. It should also be low, both so the defender can't run in and hit it in, and because a higher ball stays in the air longer and so gives the opponent more time to react to it. (You can also drop shot against an off-table lobber with a dead block or chop block, though that's more difficult to keep short.)

A short push against an attacker's serve is actually more effective if it isn't too short, but short enough so that it would bounce twice if given the chance. The problem here is that the attacker is usually at the table, and so dropping the ball very short won't catch him out of position unless he's very short or immobile. And if he's in position for the shot, the shorter ball is both easier to attack with a flip than the slightly longer one, and easier to drop short.

There are always exceptions. Against a very fast-footed defender that you can't really catch with a drop shot, you might not want to drop the ball too short as it just gives him easy balls to pick hit, especially with a running backhand smash. And against an attacker who likes to serve and step back a bit, looking for a long return, an extra-short drop shot might be effective. But as a general rule, use drop shots against choppers, and short pushes against attackers.

February 24, 2014 – Backhand Sidespin Push

When pushing on the backhand, most players are at one of three levels:

- **Level One**: Get it back.
- **Level Two**: Do something with it. This usually means one of three things: Quick off the bounce and angled; heavy; or short. This is effective at all levels. But there's another level. . . .
- **Level Three**: Do even more!

There are several examples of "more." You can aim your racket one way, and at the last instant go another, a must learn for any advanced player. You can fake heavy spin, and give no-spin by snapping the wrist vigorously just after contact. You should learn both of these. Another option is a sidespin push.

There are different types of sidespin pushes, but what we'll cover here is the most common one: the backhand sidespin push, where the racket is going right to left at contact (for a righty).

To do this shot, start with your racket a little above the ball and to the right. You want to take the ball off the bounce, so your opponent is rushed; the more time he has, the more likely he'll adjust to your sidespin. As the ball hits the table, stroke down and sideways (right to left). Some contact the ball toward the bottom of the racket, so they can take it quicker off the bounce, or you can contact in the middle of the racket for more control. The key is to put both backspin and sidespin on the ball.

Placement is important. You usually want to do this shot to the opponent's wide backhand so it breaks away from him (assuming both players are righties or both are lefties). It's a tricky ball to backhand loop, and if he tries running around to use his forehand, the sidespin pulls the ball farther to the side than he's expecting.

When a righty plays a lefty, both players have the option of using this shot so that it breaks into the wide forehand. Not only is it pulling away from the opponent, but this type of breaking away sidespin often causes more trouble to player's forehands than ones that break into the body (i.e. righty versus righty). It also puts him out of position. When a lefty serves to you (if you are a righty, or a righty serving to you if you are a lefty), and serves short to the backhand, this is an excellent return, into his wide forehand.

The down side of this shot is that, because there is less backspin, an opponent who reads it properly can loop right through the ball, often off the bounce. So you don't want to over use this shot. However, done at proper times, it's a highly effective shot. It also puts one more thing in your opponent's mind to think about.

One time this shot is especially useful is against an opponent's forehand sidespin serve (assuming two righties). You can use the opponent's sidespin against him, returning and adding to his own spin as you really sidespin your return into his wide backhand.

CHAPTER FOUR: FOOTWORK

April 27, 2015 –
Your Ready Position – Think Basketball

Many players play table tennis like they were playing pinball. They stand there, and when they have to move, they mostly just reach for the ball. The reason for this is a combination of two factors: they are *not ready to move*, and they are *not in the habit of moving*. These are two separate things.

A coach could stress the proper ready stance and the importance of moving, and try to get the player to be ready to move and to develop the habit of doing so. And it might sink in. But there's an easier way. Put your racket aside. Now imagine you are covering someone in basketball. (Or an infielder in baseball or a goalie in soccer.) Don't think about it; *just do it*. Then examine what happens. Almost for certain your feet went a little wider, your weight went on the balls of the feet, your knees bent some and pointed outwards slightly, and you leaned forward slightly at the waist. Your knees were suddenly bouncy as you prepared to move in either direction. (You probably raised your arms as well; you can drop them now, but keep the free hand up some for balance.) You are now in a perfect ready position!

You are now *ready to move*. Do this regularly, and you'll develop the *habit of moving*. Your pinball days are over.

August 10, 2015 – You Can Be Light on Your Feet

There's a myth that to be light on your feet, you have to be in great shape. It's true that being in great shape will allow you to move faster than one who is not. But this is not the same thing as being light on your feet, which is about how *quickly* you start to move, not how fast you move once you get going.

How quickly you start to move – i.e. how light you are on your feet – is mostly a technique thing. If you watch the top players or anyone who seems to move quickly, watch how they take a slight hop as the opponent is making his shot. It is this slight bounce that prepares a player to move almost instantly. Those who simply stand there, waiting to see if and where they have to move, lose the bounce that comes from this, and so they are very slow to start to move.

There are players a hundred pounds overweight or in their seventies who are light on their feet, and players in tiptop physical condition who are not. This doesn't mean they move fast; it means they get started quickly, and so while they may not cover a lot of ground, they often seem to always be in position – because they are never flat-footed and stuck in place. It means they react to shots very quickly because they are always ready to move.

Are you light on your feet? There's a simple test. When you are caught off guard, such as against a net or edge ball, do you step to the ball, or do you just reach for it? If the latter, you are flat-footed.

To see this little bounce that players do between shots, you can watch just about any video of top players, and focus on one player. You'll see this slight bounce as the opponent is hitting the ball. Few people see this because 1) it happens too fast, and 2) when watching a match, most viewers are watching whoever is hitting the ball rather than the one who is not. Ideally, see it in slow motion. Here's video of Zhang Jike doing multiball:

www.youtube.com/watch?v=BFpiU-0un1s

Or go to Youtube.com and search for "Table Tennis Training - ZHANG Jike Multi Ball & Slow Motion of Fast Footwork."

Watch seconds 45-50, and you can see (in the slow motion) the very obvious bounce he does between shots.

Or just watch video of just about any other high-level match, such as the video highlights (4:50) of the Men's Singles Final at the 2015 World Championships:

www.youtube.com/watch?v=XkzX9khxflo

Or search in Youtube.com for "WTTC 2015 Highlights: MA Long vs FANG Bo (FINAL)."

Focus on either player (Ma Long in Black, Fang Bo in orange), and watch their knees. For example, in the very first point, see how Ma

Long returns the serve, and then makes two great forehand loops. But it is the slight hop he takes before moving to each of these shots that allows him to get the quick start that positions him for these shots.

Another thing that's important is the foot positioning. To be light on your feet, use a relatively wide stance in a slight crouch, knees pointed slightly outward, with weight on the inside balls of the feet.

The thing to emphasize is that you can be overweight, old, and have bad knees, and you can still take this slight bounce – it's just a matter of making it a habit. How do you make it a habit? Like anything else – practice. But the nice thing is that this is one of those few things you can practice doing just as well in a match as in a drill, so there's no excuse for not practicing it. Just do it.

February 29, 2016 – Move Those Feet

Whether you are 8 or 80, or somewhere in between, moving your feet is a priority. It's something that coaches constantly harp on. Beginning kids often don't find it important, and so you have to drill it into them, and then they quickly pick up on it. Older players often find it difficult because of their age, but while age slows you down, it doesn't stop you from moving your feet – it's simply a habit. An older player who doesn't move fast but still moves his feet is faster than a really fast player who doesn't.

Here is Exhibit A, video of George Brathwaite (6:05) in a training session.

www.youtube.com/watch?v=AGbDDqo0CqM

Or search Youtube.com for "George Braithwaite Performing Table Tennis Drills 2015."

George "The Chief" is well into his eighties (Google "George Brathwaite Hall of Fame profile"), but see how he still moves his feet? That's because he has made it a habit. Let me emphasize this again: Moving the feet is a *habit*. It has nothing to do with how fast your feet are or how old you are.

Often players instead reach for the ball, meaning they limit their range, go off balance, and have to do an awkward stroke instead of the one they've spent so much time perfecting. The problem is they haven't developed the reaction of *stepping* to the ball, and so they instead react by reaching – which both puts them off balance and forces them to improvise the shot. Just as a person reflexively blinks if something comes at their eye, you should learn to reflexively step to wherever the ball is going. This doesn't mean you'll reach the ball every time, and sometimes you might even take that step and still have to lunge after it, but that's *only* after taking that first reflexive step. Focus on balance, with your weight centered as you move, and only going to your back foot for weight transfer as you get into position.

Some would say, "Of course George can move his feet – he's a Hall of Fame player!" But that's backwards – he's a Hall of Famer *because* he worked hard to develop such basic habits as moving his feet. George can do it in his eighties. What's your excuse?

September 21, 2015 – Recover from the Previous Shot

Table tennis is a game of movement. You'll regularly see players fail to run down a shot, and then grumble to themselves, "Too slow!" But was he really too slow, or did he fail to recover from the previous shot?

Everyone is limited by their natural foot speed. However, players who grumble about being "too slow" often have it wrong – they aren't too slow, they simply get a slow start because of a poor recovery from the previous shot.

Here are some tips that'll allow you to recover and react more quickly to an opponent's shot, allowing you to move more quickly. Do these, and your slowness of feet will be gone with the wind – or, to paraphrase a famous quote, "As the Table Tennis Gods are your witness, you'll never be slow again!"

- **Focus on balance**. If you are even slightly off-balance from the previous shot you'll have a slow recovery as you recover that balance, and so will be slow to get to the next shot. This especially happens after players do exaggerated follow-throughs on forehand shots. Try to stay balanced throughout the stroke.
- **Ready stance**. If you don't smoothly and quickly move into a good ready stance after the previous shot, you won't be ready to react to the next shot. This means feet relatively wide, weight toward the inside balls of the feet, feet pointed slightly outward, knees slightly bent, racket held out in front and aimed at the opponent.

- **Racket height**. If you hold your racket too high after the previous shot or in your regular ready position, it'll take too long to bring it down for the next shot.
- **Flex those knees**. If you don't flex them at least slightly as the opponent is hitting his shot (i.e. a mini-bounce), you'll have to do so *after* he hits his shot before you can move, which slows you down. Try to be light on your feet.
- **Clear the mind and just react**. If you try to anticipate an opponent's shot, then unless you get it exactly right every time you won't be physically or mentally ready for the next shot, which slows you down. It's better to just watch the opponent and react as soon as he's committed to a shot and direction. Learn to work with your subconscious.

September 14, 2015 – Do You Have the Blocking Reachies?

Raise your hand if you tend to reach for the ball when blocking. Don't be shy – raising your hand is like reaching for the ball, so you should be good at it!

The problem with reaching for the ball is that it means you'll have multiple blocking strokes, rather than two good ones (backhand and forehand). This doesn't mean you can't ever reach when needed, but that should be a last resort. Stepping to the ball allows you to use the same consistent blocking stroke over and over, leading to a consistent block. So let's kick this habit once and for all so you'll never reach for the ball when blocking or find yourself raising your hand while reading a coaching article.

What causes the Blocking Reachies? Several things.

1. **You have no choice but to reach if your feet are anchored to the ground**. So be light on your feet. Weight should be toward the front inside part of the feet. Bounce slightly between shots to better prepare yourself for the next shot. Even slow, out-of-shape players with bad knees can do this; it's just a habit to develop.
2. **If you wait to see if you have to move, you're wasting time**. Expect to move; it's just a matter of what direction and how far. So imagine you are on the starting blocks, and take off as soon as you see where the ball is going.

3. **Moving is a habit**. Players who think they aren't fast enough to move are mistaking a bad habit for slowness. The instant you see where the ball is going your reaction should be to step in that direction. You can begin a step just as fast as you can begin a reach. If necessary, do both, just don't skip the stepping part. One way to make this a habit is to shadow stroke the footwork. Imagine a ball coming to you to your right or left, and practice stepping to it to block. Do this over and over until it's a habit. Focus on balance as you move. And don't rush; in most cases you have more time than you think.

Develop confidence in your blocking, knowing that you can cover the entire table with a single step in either direction, and turn yourself into the Great Wall of You.

December 15, 2014 – Backhand Footwork

Many players do lots and lots of forehand footwork drills. This allows many of them to dominate the table with their forehand. But there's often a missing ingredient here – backhand footwork.

Backhand footwork is similar to forehand footwork – you need to learn to move side to side as well as in and out. For example, a coach or partner simply hits the ball side to side to the backhand side, one toward the middle, one to the corner or wider. The player moves side to side, playing backhands. Players who don't do this often have trouble covering the backhand side effectively. They can move all over the forehand court fluidly, but on the backhand side they are in trouble. Often this means either weak and erratic backhands, or wild swats.

Often coaches don't work on this much. Why? First, the forehand tends to be the stronger shot, and so coaches and players stress that – and so do lots of forehand footwork drills. Second, many forehand footwork drills incorporate backhands as part of the drill, and so they do get some backhand footwork practice this way, and so think they are doing sufficient backhand footwork drills. However, most of these drills only cover moving from the forehand side to the backhand side, not just moving around on the backhand side itself. Third, by the time players reach the intermediate stage they have developed forehands and so are doing lots of forehand footwork drills – but often the backhand isn't as developed, and so coaches have them focus on continued technique development rather than moving about playing backhand. Many intermediate players are making the transition from normal backhand drives to topspinning their backhands, and coaches are reluctant to have them work on this and do footwork at the same time. (This one doesn't apply to coaches who introduce forehand and backhand topspin shots to developing players at about the same time, as more and more modern coaches tend to do.) And fourth, by the time the player does have a solid topspin backhand, both the coach and the player aren't in the habit of doing backhand footwork drills in their sessions, and so they just don't do them.

All this can lead to a weakness in the player's game as they don't move around as well as they could in covering the backhand side. This is a problem as the backhand by its very nature is a more cramped shot, with the body in the way, and so being able to move about and attack with the backhand is key.

Besides side-to-side backhand footwork, you can also try in and out. Ideally, learn to topspin from both positions, but especially from off the table. You should also do random backhand footwork, where balls are played randomly to the backhand and you play aggressive backhands. You can also have your coach or partner attack randomly to your backhand so you can work on your backhand blocking footwork, or perhaps topspin defend from a few steps back.

Eric Owens attributed his upset win over Cheng Yinghua in Men's Singles at the 2001 USA Nationals to backhand footwork drills. Learn from the champions!

May 11, 2015 – Covering the Wide Backhand

Playing backhands at the start of a rally is easy, since you are in position. But what do you do when you've been moved to your wide forehand, and have to move quickly to cover the wide backhand? You have three movement options – diagonally in, diagonally sideways, and diagonally back.

1. **Diagonally In**. For this, you would move in to cut the ball off quickly, before it has a chance to get past you. If you are a close to the table player, then this is what you'd want to do. You also might want to do this if you were moved off the table when covering the forehand; moving in gets you back to the table. By moving in and taking the ball more quickly, you rush the opponent, or at least don't give him time to wind up for his next shot. When moving in like this, most players block or drive the ball. At the advanced levels players can move in and backhand loop the ball, often on the rise. The downside of moving in, of course, is that you have little time, and so either simply don't have time to do so, or are rushed and so make mistakes. You don't want to rush your shots, so only move in if you have time, or if you are doing a relatively simple block.

2. **Diagonally Sideways**. This is the most common way, and what I'd recommend for most players. This gives you time to do your best backhand shot, whether driving or looping, without backing up so much that your opponent has too much time. If you want to improve, you should endlessly practice moving side-to-side where you move mostly sideways. Many players may have a small diagonally in movement when covering the backhand because most players tend to take the ball quicker on the backhand side than the forehand, but if it's only a little, then it's essentially sideways.

3. **Diagonally Back**. This is a defensive method, and should normally be done only when absolutely forced to. Players who strongly favor the forehand often find themselves rushing about playing the forehand, and when moved to the wide forehand, often have to back up to cover the wide backhand. If you are forced back in this way, you will most likely be spinning soft with the backhand or fishing, or (if really in trouble) chopping or lobbing. (If your style of play is chopping, then there's nothing wrong with this. But if you are an attacker who is forced to chop because of this, then you are probably at a disadvantage if forced to chop.) If you find yourself forced back in this way on the wide backhand, there are two things to consider. First, try and make your shot as effective as possible, given the circumstances – and that mostly means keeping your ball deep, ideally with good topspin. Second, consider what got you into this situation in the first place, and find ways to avoid this situation.

May 31, 2016 – How to Cover a Short Ball to the Forehand

These days many players try to receive these with their backhands, often using a backhand banana flip. (See www.tabletenniscoaching.com/node/1311.) And there's nothing wrong with doing that. However, you'll run into problems if you can't also flip return these with your forehand – an opponent might use the same motion and either serve short to the forehand or long to the backhand, and unless you have world-class feet, you aren't going to be covering both with your backhand. So learn to return these shots with your forehand as well, with flips and pushes.

The key is stepping in properly. For right-handers, that means stepping in with the right foot as far in as needed. Balance is key, so keep your left arm out in the opposite direction, like a fencer doing an "en garde."

But you can't really learn this just by doing it when it's needed; you need to systematically practice it. This means:

- Shadow practicing the shot until it's second nature. Perhaps even put a mark on the floor under the table where the right foot should go, and another where it should be in your regular stance, and then move back and forth, while also shadow-stroking a flip or push when you step in.
- Practicing it with a partner or coach. Have him serve short to your forehand, or you serve short and he drops it short there, and then you can step in to practice the shot. Even better, do it with multiball, where the coach/practice partner alternates one ball short to the forehand (usually backspin or no-spin), another somewhere else (either random, or perhaps long to the backhand).
- Then do it in game situations. Perhaps play games where both players have to serve short to the forehand, so both get practice on this.

Once you have confidence in receiving short balls with the forehand, you can do so either forehand or backhand, depending on the situation. And if you have a good forehand, you'll find that you might even want to receive with the forehand sometimes against short balls to the middle or even backhand, as it puts you in perfect position to follow with a big forehand!

CHAPTER FIVE: TACTICS

GENERAL

December 1, 2014 – What's Your Game Plan?

Do you have a game plan when you play? Or do you just wing it and hope?

Many players mostly wing it, to their detriment. Most have patterns they use, but often they haven't really thought them through. Every serve and receive should have purpose; otherwise, you are playing without purpose. Often the plans they do have don't take into consideration the opponent's strengths and weaknesses. For example, if you are a looper, you probably have patterns to set up your loop, but how much do you focus on adjusting these techniques and your loop itself (placement, speed, spin, etc.) to your opponent?

What is the strongest part of your game? What is your opponent's weakest? How can you connect these two? Failing that, how can you get your strength against your opponent's average, or perhaps your average against your opponent's weakness? You need to be looking for ways to force these match-ups.

If you have a good serve and loop, it's not enough to serve and loop; you have to know where to serve and loop. For example, I'm forever reminding players with good loops that they normally shouldn't just loop to the backhand, and then look for a chance to attack the middle or wide forehand, where most players are weaker defensively. Why not plan to attack the middle first? (At the higher levels, against a very good counterlooper who is waiting, you might not want to do this – but often they are hanging around their backhand side, leaving the wide forehand somewhat open. And yet, even at that level, the middle is usually the weakest spot.)

Think about someone you regularly play against. What is he uncomfortable against? You might want to consider how others play against him, since it's possible you are missing his problem areas. Then figure out how you can best match up against him.

But don't think of it as just one tactical solution to one player. The key is to make it a *habit* to develop game plans – something you automatically think about and implement every time you play. When game plans become a habit you'll get your better shots into play while picking apart the weaknesses of your opponents, leading to more upsets, beating your peers, and dominating against weaker players who might have given you problems before.

December 27, 2016 – Focus on How to Beat Someone, Not On Why You Can't

How often have you played a match against someone who has something that scares you? Strong serves? Strong forehand or backhand? Quick blocks? Heavy push? And so on. Many players get pre-occupied worrying about how to deal with these shots rather than focusing on what they can do to win.

For example, if an opponent has a very strong backhand, don't focus on or worry about their backhand; instead focus on what you want to do to bring your own strong shots out while avoiding theirs. Against a strong backhand player, you have many options. You can attack their forehand; go to the forehand to draw them out of position and then go back to their backhand, forcing awkward shots; go to the middle and wide backhand (as well as forehand) to force even more awkward shots; keep the ball deep so their backhands aren't so strong; give them shots that their backhand isn't so strong against (heavy topspin, heavy backspin, quick shots, etc.); throw them off with varied pace; or use serve and receive to dominate rallies so they don't get to use their strong backhand (or whatever else their strength is).

The same is true of any other strong shot, including serves. If they have a strong serve, focus on how to return it to take away their best follow ups. So stop worrying, do some analysis, perhaps experiment a bit, and focus on bringing out your strong shots while taking away the opponent's!

May 4, 2015 – Good Tactics Lead to Confidence

Think about the last time you played a match and got nervous. Now ask yourself this: What were your tactics in that match? If you are like the overwhelming majority of players I've worked with over the years in that situation, you probably didn't have a strong game plan – you were probably just winging it. And so, unsure of what you were doing, you were (drum roll please) . . . unsure of what you were doing. And it is that lack of surety that often leads to nervousness.

So next time you are nervous, ask yourself what your game plan is, and come up with a coherent one. Not only will this give your mind something to think about other than worrying about your upcoming doom, but it will give you the confidence that you know what you are doing. You still have to execute the shots, but it's a lot easier to be confident when you know what you are doing than when you don't. Plus, this confidence allows you to think a bit more clearly and so play even better tactics. In other words:

Good Tactics => Confidence => Even Better Tactics => Even More Confidence

Let's break this down. Suppose you get nervous in a match. Rather than just tell yourself not to be nervous, think tactically. Ask yourself what tactics you need to do to win. Keep it simple – that is key. Then execute those tactics in a flexible way. (Flexible as in be ready for anything, but use tactics to increase the chances of the rallies going the way you want them.) If you focus on simple tactics and execution, you may find the nervousness melting away as you've given your mind something simple to focus on. This leads to confidence and a clear mind, which leads to clear thinking and continued good tactical play, which leads to even more confidence. It's an upward spiral that leads to playing your best – or, as it's often called, playing "In the Zone."

When I talk to players after losses, often they'll blame their loss on nervousness. It's only when I question them that the whole truth comes out!

June 20, 2016 – Always Have at Least Two Options

Many players have multiple options for most situations, but only one for some. For example, against a deep, spinny serve to the backhand, many players will only backhand drive it crosscourt. Or against a backspin serve to the backhand will almost always push it crosscourt. (Crosscourtitis is a curse many players have – there is such a thing as down the line, and you should learn to use it.)

When you have only one option off something the opponent does, then the opponent no longer has to worry about anything but that one option. And since a player with only one option usually only has that one option because he's not particularly comfortable with the incoming shot, it usually means the one option he uses isn't very strong. But even if it is, it loses its effectiveness when the opponent knows it's coming.

Even if the opponent isn't a "thinking" opponent, i.e. one who figures out opponent's weaknesses (such as predictability), most players are instinctive, and subconsciously pick up on these things. They may not realize it at the time, but they often are reacting to this predictableness.

So examine your game, and find places where you generally do the same thing over and over. It's possible that this works against some players, or even most players your level – but it probably *doesn't* work against stronger players, and presumably they are the ones you are hoping to learn to beat. So make sure that in every situation, you have at least two options.

Here's an example. During my playing career I often liked to give big breaking sidespin serves deep to the backhand, so that the ball would break to my right, away from the righty's backhand. Most would reach for the ball and make moderately aggressive shots to my backhand – but I'd already be over there, just waiting for this shot with my forehand. The ones that gave me trouble would either take it down the line – often doing so a bit more quickly and catching me – or would simply mix in a chop now and then, which would completely throw me off, since I was generally a step back, waiting for that topspin return.

June 9, 2014 – Controlling a Match (Version 1)

Controlling a match means forcing the rallies to go the way you want them to. In general, that means hitters hit, loopers loop, blockers block, and so on. How to you go about doing this?

There are two basic ways of controlling a match. One is to develop a style where you can force your strengths on your opponent. The other way is to develop an all-around style that adjusts to your opponent so that you can play on his weaknesses. In both cases it is your serve and receive that will often allow you to take control.

1. Forcing Your Strengths on an Opponent

First you must develop or identify your strengths. Once those are developed, you need to develop your game, especially your serve and receive game, so as to put these strengths into play. All options have advantages and disadvantages.

For example, if you serve short backspin, it'll often be pushed long, allowing a looper to loop, and allowing a hitter to loop to set up his hitting. But it might also be pushed short, or pushed quick and aggressively off the bounce at a wide angle, or flipped, and any of these three might give the receiver control of the point. So you might vary this by serving short sidespin or no-spin serves that look like backspin, and watch the receiver struggle against the varying spin (or no-spin).

If you serve long (either fast or with a breaking sidespin), you might get a soft topspin return that you can loop or hit. But it risks letting the opponent loop, which can put a looper or hitter on the defensive and the receiver in control. However, an awkward or weak loop by the receiver might set up a quick blocker.

Better still, use both types of serves, and by varying them, completely dominate the poor receiver, who can never adjust to your constantly varying serves.

How do you force your strengths on the opponent when he's serving? See the previous examples, but from the receiver's point of view. Take control of the point against short serves by dropping them short, pushing aggressively, and flipping. Against deep serves, attack. Use placement and variation to take control of the point.

2. Playing on Your Opponent's Weaknesses

The other option is to develop an all-around style where you can play to the opponent's weaknesses. For example, if the opponent isn't very fast, you might adopt a blocking game, and quick-block side to side.

Use your serve and receive to force these types of rallies, perhaps with deep serves that force topspin returns you can quick-block.

Or if the opponent has trouble blocking against slow, spinny loops, serve short and get ready to loop any long push returns. If the opponent doesn't have a good put-away shot, then you might combine a steady game with sudden attacks, knowing you can take your time and pick your shots since the opponent isn't a threat to end the point. If your opponent has a strong forehand but weaker backhand, you might simply play everything wide to his backhand. If he's the type that plays his forehand from the backhand side, then perhaps go to the forehand first (perhaps with a short serve, an aggressive receive, or a quick block), then come back to the backhand and pin him down there.

There's also a psychology to controlling a match. You have certain tools in your tactical toolbox, i.e. your entire arsenal of shots (serves, receives, strokes, footwork). Think of your racket as your magic wand, and use it to completely dominate an opponent with these tools, and have the confidence to do so. If you don't have the tools to do this, then it's time to think about your game and what new tools you need, and to develop them.

August 17, 2015 – Controlling a Match (Version 2)

A match doesn't always go to the player with the best shots. Just as often it goes to the player who knows how to control play. It doesn't matter how strong the opponent's shots may be if he rarely gets a chance to use them effectively. How do you do this?

You control a match primarily with serve and receive, which sets up your first shot in the rally. When choosing these shots you should ask yourself three questions:

1. **What serve/receive is your opponent weakest against?**
   This is the most obvious and needs little explaining. It's also the most overused, as opponents expect this, and develop ways to overcome these weaknesses. This doesn't mean you shouldn't pound your opponent on his weaknesses, but if that's the limit of your tactics, you'll have trouble controlling a match against many players.

2. **What serve/receive will put your opponent into a weak position?**

    Sometimes this overlaps with #1 above, but not always. For example, a player may have a very good forehand flip against a short serve to the forehand, but it draws him over the table, and if he's weaker on the backhand, it might leave him open on that side. So you might sometimes serve short to the forehand, and prepare to block his flip to his backhand, and then take control of the rally. Or, against a strong forehand player, sometimes challenge his forehand by serving deep there, and quick block to the weaker backhand side, and take control of the rally. (The reverse of both of these also works, where you serve to the backhand and block to the forehand.)

    The same idea works when receiving. For example, a player may have a strong forehand loop against backspin, but if you aim your receive to the forehand, and then at the last second instead quick push to the backhand, it takes away the opponent's forehand loop and puts him in a weak position. In general, if an opponent is strong on one side but weaker on the other, you might want to go wide to the strong side first, then quick block to the weak side, catching the opponent out of position and forced to use his weaker side while moving or reaching.

3. **What serve/receive is your opponent not expecting?**

    This is probably the most underused tactic. If a player has trouble with a certain serve, receive, or shot, he'll likely be expecting it. While you should still pound him on this weakness, you'll do even better if you regularly catch him off guard with the unexpected. Examples are endless – you simply vary all of your serves, receives, and shots to keep the opponent off guard, forcing erratic or weaker returns, and then take control of the rally. But there are a number of standard combinations that can keep an opponent guessing. For example, using the same serving motion, serve either short to the forehand with varying spins (including no-spin), or deep, breaking serves to the backhand. The opponent doesn't know if he's got to be ready to step in for the short serve to the forehand or cover the wide, deep backhand. Then throw in a few other serves, such as a fast no-spin to the middle, and watch the opponent wither.

This tactic is also way underused when receiving. Far too many players receive predictably over and over rather than catch the opponent off guard. This is often because a player doesn't have confidence in more than one type of receive against a given serve – but rather than resigning himself to mediocrity, why not develop a full range of receives, so that you can both receive in the way the opponent has the most trouble against (#1 above), as well as being able to vary the receive and so leaving your opponent never knowing what to expect?

Always remember – whoever has the bigger serve & receive arsenal – and knows how to use it to control play – usually wins.

February 1, 2016 – Holding Back Against a Weaker Player

A common problem when facing a weaker player is literally going into the match with the tactical plan of not playing your best. Rather than play your normal attacking shots, you play soft, hoping not to risk the more difficult shots that make you the better player. It's often a mistake.

This doesn't mean you should be ripping shots left and right against a player where you could win without taking such risks. But if you are used to mostly attacking at a certain range of speeds off a given shot, and hold back on this to play "safe," you're more likely to both miss the shot while giving the opponent an easier shot to respond to. Holding back usually means you take conscious control of a shot to soften the shot for "safety," which means you are throwing away much of the muscle memory you've trained so hard to develop. Result? You play soft and erratic, and the opponent has shots to tee off against while not facing your best shots, the very ones that made you the better player. *That* is risky play.

So it's usually best to just play your game against a weaker player, focusing on the type of tactics that will allow you to play your best game without playing overly safe or risky. By doing so from the start, you spread the "risk" over the entire match, and guess what? While individually some of these aggressive shots might be "risky," the risk goes away if spread out over an entire match. If you would normally loop a given ball rather hard, then do so, and let the muscle memory guide you.

July 21, 2014 – Overplaying and Underplaying

Two of the most common reasons players don't play their best are overplaying and underplaying. Overplaying is when a player goes for shots that are beyond his level, such as trying to rip winners over and over rather than use more consistent opening attacks to set up easier winners (as well as winning a surprising number of points outright as opponents miss against your steady opening attack). Underplaying is the opposite – when a player plays too safe. Both of these often take place when a player is nervous. Under pressure, many players do one or the other, either getting wildly aggressive or too safe. The key is to find the right balance.

The way to develop a high-level attack isn't to rip every ball; it's to attack at the level you are consistent, and keep working to increase that level until you have a high-level attack. Way too many players want to rip that first ball when, if they'd take just a little off the shot, they'd be far more consistent and on the path to improvement. Top players may rip the ball harder on the first shot, but that's because they are farther along that road to improvement – they've put in the hours of developing that shot. So should you. So focus on making strong first attacks, and perhaps rip the *next* ball. A good general rule is this – until you have an easy pop-up, never attack at more than 80% speed.

The reverse are the players who have developed strong attacks, but are afraid to use them. If that's you, then the key is to simply learn to use those attack shots you've worked so hard to develop. If you can't do it in a tournament, perhaps work your way up to that. First use them in practice or league matches, especially against weaker players. Then against players your own level. When you can do that, then start using them in tournaments. If you have difficulty doing that, then the answer might be to play a series of tournaments in a row. That way you'll get used to playing tournament matches. You might only have to do this one time, i.e. find a series of weekends where you can play tournament after tournament, until you get used to it, and using the shots you do in practice becomes more natural to do in tournaments. Once you can do this one time, it's a habit you should be able to keep for a lifetime, at least as long as you practice enough to keep the shots in practice.

So a key to table tennis is that you not only have to develop your shots, you have to use them at the proper level, without over- or under-playing them, and keep developing your game so that this middle area gets better and better.

October 24, 2016 – Winning Cheap Points

Cheap points are when you do something seemingly simple, often subtle, and force the opponent into an error. For example, you might push a serve back extra heavy, and the opponent loops into the net. Or, after serving short several times in a row, you serve fast at the receiver's middle, catching him off guard, and again get an easy point. Or a last-second change of direction. Or a suddenly well-placed dead block. There are many possibilities.

The problem is that most players are so focused on either ripping winners or keeping the ball in play that they don't develop the instincts to win these cheap points. Most of what they do is predictable, and while they may rip lots of winners and keep the ball in play, so does the opponent.

How do you learn to win such cheap points? Experiment, observe the result, and learn. This doesn't mean playing all sorts of weird shots; it means trying out different things and seeing what works – a last-second change of direction, an unexpected change of spin, a change-of-pace block, and so on. These are the type of things that win cheap points for you by your opponent missing or making a weak shot. You can also win cheap points on your serve by throwing in an occasional "trick" serve.

On the following page are some of my favorite ways to win a "cheap" point:

Ways to Win a "Cheap" Point

1. Sudden fast serves, either breaking into wide backhand, no-spin to the middle (receiver's playing elbow), or quick down the line.

2. After several backspin serves, a side-top or no-spin serve, but with a big downward follow through.

3. Quick blocks and other attacks to the opponent's middle.

4. Set up to loop crosscourt from forehand, at the last second rotate the shoulders back and go down the line.

5. Set up to loop crosscourt from the backhand, at the last second whip the shoulders around and go down the line.

6. Backhand loops that go down the line or at the elbow instead of the normal crosscourt ones.

7. Aim a backhand crosscourt, then at the last second bring the wrist back and go down the line.

8. Against short backspin, sudden very aggressive and angled pushes.

9. Aim a push to the right, at the last second drop the racket tip and push to the left. Can be done short or long.

10. Take a shot right off the bounce, throwing opponent's timing off. This can be done against serves or other shots, with quick drives, blocks, or pushes.

11. Dead blocks that mess up opponent's timing. They can be no-spin, or chop blocks and sidespin blocks.

12. Suddenly aggressive dead block, especially if you pin the opponent on the backhand.

13. Slow spinny loops that drop short, near the net. Opponents often mistime them if they hesitate.

14. No-spin "Dummy" loops. Exaggerate the normal looping motion but use no wrist.

15. When fishing and lobbing, vary the height, placement, and spin of the shots.

16. Place your weak shots. If you have to make a weak return, at least make the opponent move! Perhaps aim one way then go the other to catch the opponent off guard.

July 20, 2015 – The Tricky Side of Table Tennis

Here are ten tricky things you can do win a few points here and there – as well as make the game more interesting!

1. **Muscle-Tensing Ball Clench.** When hiding the ball under the table at the start of a match to see who serves first, subtly clench the muscles in the hand not holding the ball, and you're opponent will likely choose that hand, giving you the choice of serve, receiver, or side.

2. **The Left-Right Shuffle.** This is for when you are playing someone who will almost for certain push your serve back, and who will push to your wide forehand if you leave it open. (We'll assume both players are righties for this.) You serve backspin to their backhand, and then, before the opponent hits the ball, you step to your left as if you are looking for a forehand from the backhand corner. Then, just as the receiver is predictably pushing to your open forehand, you step that way and have an easy forehand loop.

3. **The Server Stare.** As you are serving look intently at one spot, but serve to another spot.

4. **Ready Position Switch.** As the opponent serves, change your ready position. You can vary from a neutral position, a backhand position, or a forehand position.

5. **Funky Serves.** There's nothing like a weird serve to throw an opponent off. For example, did you know it's legal to serve off the back of your hand? The racket is considered to include your playing hand below the wrist. Or make any weird or "funky" move as you serve. Some Japanese players are infamous for rather weird arm contortions as they serve. Or just develop some sort of rare serve that might not be so effective on its own, but because they don't see it often, if you use it sparingly it becomes effective.

6. **Varying Bounce Serve.** Before serving, bounce the ball on the table a number of times, as many top players do. Most of the time do the same number of bounces – say, five – and then quickly serve. Then, at a key moment, only bounce it once, and then quickly serve. It may throw off your opponent's timing.

7. **Fake Loop**. When an opponent pushes, wind up as if you are going for a big loop, but at the last second push. Your opponent will likely be getting set to block, and so will be caught off guard by this.

8. **Dummy Loop**. Loop the ball, but keep your wrist up so there's little snap into the shot. Exaggerate your follow-through. The ball will look spinny but will be relatively dead, and your opponent will likely struggle to adjust or he'll go into the net.

9. **Dummy Push**. Push, but use no wrist at contact, and just pat the ball back rather than spin it. Right after contact do a big wrist snap. The push will look spinny but will be nearly spinless, and the opponent will likely pop it up or go off the end.

10. **Last-Second Changes**. With any shot, aim one way, and change directions at the last second. This is especially effective with short, quick shots, such as pushes and blocks, but also works for other shots, including loops.

March 23, 2015 – Macho or Tricky?

One of the toughest decisions a player has to make when serving under pressure – or at any other time – is whether to go "macho" or "tricky."

Going macho means you serve mostly to set up a third-ball attack, knowing that you will have to follow your serve up with a strong attack. Most often these serves will give you a return you can attack, but receivers generally don't miss these serves outright, and you will have to make a good shot or sequence of shots to win the point.

Going tricky means pulling out a serve where you are trying to win the point outright with the serve, either by the receiver missing the serve or giving an easy pop-up. The weakness of these serves is that if the receiver reads them well, they are often easier to attack then third-ball serves. They tend to be all or nothing serves, where either the receiver misses, or the receiver attacks the serve. (Of course, if the opponent plays passively, then things are different – challenge them over and over with trick serves, since there's little danger of them attacking them.)

So which should you choose? First off, you should have complete confidence that you can win by going "macho," knowing that you can follow up your serve. At the world-class level, these serves dominate. At the same time, you want to play the percentages – that's all tactics is, playing the percentages, and so that's all you should be thinking about here. You can't put an exact percentage on it, but you should be asking yourself, "Do I have a serve he keeps missing?"

Sometimes you might even have a serve you haven't used yet, and pull it out at the end – but I don't recommend that. If it's such a good serve that it should win you a point, use it earlier, both to win the point and to verify it'll work. If it does, then hold back on it for a time until the opponent isn't ready, then pull it out again. Why pull out a tricky serve at deuce when you could pull it out early in the game and perhaps again in the middle (and perhaps not go to deuce), and again late in the game if needed?

Some players prefer to go to simple "macho" third-ball serves under pressure because they are more likely to give predictable returns, which simplifies things. And most of your serves should be of this type, with the trick serves thrown in for a few free points.

So it's all about the percentages. With experience, you'll get a feel for which type of serve to pull out in those pressure-packed moments.

February 9, 2015 – Pulling Off Big Upsets

While I always urge players to compete to win events, let's face it – one of the great thrills of table tennis is pulling off a great upset. So let's look at how to maximize your chances of doing so.

First, let's define "great upset" as beating someone who really is much better than you. If you've improved a lot and beat someone rated a lot higher only because you are underrated, that's not really a "great upset"; that just means you've gotten better. And that, of course, is better than pulling off a one-time great upset!

But whatever your current level is, you still want to maximize your chances of pulling off an occasional big upset. How do you do this? There are three main reasons why big upsets take place. They are: 1) the weaker player plays great; 2) the stronger player plays poorly; and 3) the weaker player wins because of a style advantage.

Note that tactical play comes into play in all three. The weaker player may play "well" because of smart tactics, the stronger player may play "poorly" because of poor tactics, and the weaker player may have a style advantage only because he plays smart tactics to make use of that style advantage, or because the stronger player plays poor tactics.

The reality is that most major upsets involve at least a little of all three. You have control over only how well you play, and so a key to pulling off upsets is to simply play well, so that opportunistically you are ready to win if the stronger player opens the door by playing poorly, or if it turns out you have some sort of style advantage.

Let's look at all three of these aspects.

1) Weaker Player Playing Well

Some would argue that the key to beating stronger players is to play super-aggressively and hope you get hot. This rarely works, and usually just makes things easier for the stronger player. What does work is to simply do whatever you do best, but do it as well as you can – while at the same time having at least one shot that consistently wins points against the stronger player. You don't need to force the winning shot over and over; if you do, you'll just start missing. But it needs to be there when you need it, and you should maximize how often you can use it. It might not be a one-shot putaway; it might be a series of shots, such as an aggressive backhand, quick blocking, or steady looping.

Psychologically, you need to go into the match really believing you can win. You really should do this in all matches, no matter how good the opponent is. Even if you can't beat someone, you'll do a lot better if you play believing you can, and play accordingly. This puts you in a perfect mental condition to win – you won't start thinking about the big upset you are about to pull off (and thereby fall apart) because you'll be *expecting* to win.

You also need to get into "The Zone," that mental place where you are playing almost unconsciously, where everything happens naturally. Most players have had this experience sometime; the key is to reproduce it while playing. Once in the "The Zone," you can maximize your level and your chances of winning.

It doesn't matter whether you are about to pull off a big upset because the opponent is playing poorly, you are playing well, or if you have a style advantage; in all three cases if you start to think about the upset you are about to pull off, you will likely be pulled out of the "zone" you were in, and your level of play will drop.

2) Stronger Player Playing Poorly

You can maximize the chances of the stronger player not playing well by throwing variations at him. If you give him the same serves, receives, and rallying shots over and over, he'll get used to them, get into a rhythm, and mostly likely play at his level. So perhaps throw more variations than normal against him, especially with your serves, and keep him off balance. It's a common way to blow a match, where a player finds something that works, but so overuses it that it stops working. You want to stick with what works, but you also want to stretch it out so it lasts the entire match. At the same time, once you find something that works, you want to maximize its usage without overusing it so that he gets used to it. It's a fine balance.

If you do find something that gives the stronger player trouble, here's a simple way to maximize its usage without wearing it out: use it early in a game, again in the middle, and then come back to it at the end. Often I've seen players hold back on a tricky serve, a heavy push, or something else until it's close, when if they used this earlier, the game might never be close.

3) Style Advantage

If you have a style advantage, you also maximize your chances of winning if you go in truly believing you can win. Psychologically, when you are about to beat a stronger player it's very easy to start thinking about it and thereby fall apart. Instead, if you really have a style that gives the stronger player problems, convince yourself of the truth: he is not a "stronger" player, except perhaps against other players – and he's not playing other players, he's playing *you*!

However, one of the things about stronger players is that they often adjust. This means you also need to make adjustments as the match goes on to keep that style advantage. If there's something you do that gives the stronger player problems, he'll likely look for ways to avoid that, even if it means playing his "B" game. Your job is to either find ways to keep using whatever gives him trouble, or to find ways to beat his "B" game. In the latter case, your style advantage has already done its job, forcing the stronger player to play this "B" game, and suddenly he might not necessarily be the "stronger player."

A key aspect of having a style advantage is knowing what gives the stronger player trouble, so you can use that part of your style that does give him trouble, i.e. the style advantage. Sometimes this will happen automatically, if your styles just happens to be one that gives him fits. More often it helps to do a little scouting, and find out what gives that player problems. Watch him play, ask around, experiment early in the match, and learn all you can. Information is power, and often leads to victory.

There are few more tactical matches than a clash that occurs when a stronger player faces a weaker player with a style advantage. Can he tactically adjust? Can the weaker player tactically keep using whatever it is in his style that works, or force the stronger player into his "B" game? Matches like this is where you need to put on your tactical cap and win the tactical battle. At the same time, remember that tactics should be simple. Don't overthink; find a few simple tactics that work, adjust them as needed as the match goes on, and focus on playing your best.

January 19, 2015 – The Lost Art of Messing People Up

When I throw chop blocks or sidespin pushes at my students, they complain, saying "Nobody does that!" And that's the problem – few players do these type of things anymore, and so when faced with shots that mess them up, instead of learning to do these shots themselves they point out that nobody does it – and so *nobody* does it!

Why don't players do these type of shots very often? Because the very best players in the world only do these shots occasionally. But that's because the players they are competing against are also the very best players in the world, and if you are one of the best players in the world, you have fewer problems with these types of shots. And yet many top players still do these type of shots. At the finals of Men's Singles at the recent USA Nationals, down 5-1 in the seventh, Jim Butler did three sidespin blocks the rest of the way, and won all three points. And if you watch the top players when they push serves back long, you'll be surprised at how often they do so with sidespin.

Sure, you could robotically attack every ball with the same straightforward shots that everyone uses. Or you could get a little creative, and mess up your opponents, and become a better player. It's great fun – both the messing up opponents and becoming a better player!

Here are some ways to mess up an opponent. (There are Tips of the Week that cover all of these items, either in this volume or the first one.)

1. Chop or sidespin block.
2. Push long with sidespin, usually so the ball curves out to the corners.
3. Last-second changes of direction with pushes.
4. Dummy loop, i.e. a loop that looks spinny but isn't.
5. Changing direction at the last second when looping.
6. Attack the middle.
7. Mess them up with deep, tricky serves.
8. Vary your receive against short backspin serves.

SERVICE TACTICS

November 23, 2015 – When Playing an Unfamiliar Player, Focus on Serve & Receive

When you face a new and unknown opponent, you aren't sure yet how the rallies are going to go. But you can control how the rallies start. Learn to use serve & receive to start rallies the way you want them to go, and so rather than you adjusting to your opponent, he has to adjust to you. It doesn't matter if the opponent plays very orthodox or has an unusual or weird style, you should be able to at least start the type of rally that favors you. A few examples:

- If you are good at attacking backspin, then a short, heavy, and very low backspin serve often forces a backspin return that you can attack.
- A short and low no-spin serve, as a variation to spin serves (especially backspin serves), is hard to either attack or push heavy, often giving you an easy ball to attack.
- If you serve a lot of short backspin serves and your opponent keeps pushing them back heavy, throw in short side-top serves and you'll likely get pop-ups.
- If you are good in fast topspin rallies, then a topspin or sidespin-topspin serve often forces a topspin return that you can attack. Mix them up with big breaking side-top serves as well as short ones.

- Fast & deep serves, strategically placed, often get you into a fast exchange, and can back players slightly off the table, giving you time to set up your attack. Forehand loopers are often forced out of position by these serves. Focus especially on side-top serves that break away from the receiver, fast no-spin at the elbow, and sudden quick ones down the line.
- Slow but deep sidespin serves, against an opponent who doesn't loop, sets you up for all sorts of attacks.
- If your opponent keeps attacking your short serve with his backhand, serve from the middle or forehand side so you have an angle to serve into his forehand, and force him to receive forehand.

February 17, 2014 – Fifth-Ball Attack

Most players know what a third-ball attack is: you serve, the opponent returns, and you attack aggressively, usually with a loop, a smash, a hard-hit drive, or perhaps a quick off-the-bounce drive. It's that simple. But this means you are relying on your opponent to return your serve in a way that you can attack effectively. While you want to develop your third-ball attack, you also want to develop your fifth-ball attack as your fallback plan.

What is a fifth-ball attack? You've probably already figured it out: you serve, opponent returns, you attack in a way to set up your next shot, opponent returns, and you attack aggressively (often with a smash or loop kill).

A fifth-ball attack often is just a third-ball attack with one more shot. But if your opponent is making your third-ball attack difficult, you might want to vary it with an aggressive shot that's more difficult for your opponent to stop you from doing, which sets up the next shot.

In the "classic" fifth-ball attack, you serve backspin, opponent pushes back deep, you slow- or medium-speed loop, opponent blocks, and you end the point with a smash or loop kill.

A deep, spinny loop is difficult to return without setting up your next shot. Depth is often most important – a slow loop that lands short on the opponent's side is easy to attack. (The exception to this is against a counterlooper who's too far off the table to react quickly to a slow loop that lands short.) A deep loop is much harder to return effectively. Plus, the very slowness of your slow loop gives you time to get into position for the next shot. This is why you can slow loop from the backhand corner with your forehand, and still be in position for the next shot, even if you aren't very fast.

Placement is key. The best place is often right at the opponent's middle, the transition point between forehand and backhand, usually right at the playing elbow. This forces them to make a quick decision between forehand and backhand, and often leads to a weak or inconsistent return. Or go wide to the corners if the opponent has trouble covering them. A deep, spinny loop to the very wide backhand can often cause havoc.

Many players have trouble serving and looping if their opponent pushes the serve back very heavy. This may mess up your third-ball attack, but it plays right into your fifth-ball attack. Use their backspin against them; let the ball drop slightly more than usual, and then really topspin away with a slow loop. In fact, sometimes don't even look for a third-ball "attack"; decide in advance that, unless you get an easy ball, you will serve and slow loop. This will help make your slow loop even more consistent, since there's no indecision.

Finally, remember that you don't have to force a put-away with the fifth ball. If the shot isn't there, don't go for it; just play another aggressive shot if possible, and focus on the next ball, and so on.

August 31, 2015 – How to Serve to the Backhand Attacking Receiver

One of the most difficult and often frustrating players to play is the one who seems able to attack all of your serves at will, even short backspin serves. In your attempt to get the attack, you might serve short backspin serves, but he just reaches in and backhand flips them.

You could just accept this, and play rallies with him, where each rally on your serve starts with you having to counter-attack off his backhand flip. But that means giving up your serve advantage – and since you still have to face your opponent's serves, it's likely a losing tactic. However, there's a better way of looking at this. You can't stop him from attacking your serves, but you can make him miss a good percentage of them. How to do this? There are three main ways.

First, you challenge him with extremely low and heavy backspin serves, with a few no-spin serves thrown in to mess him up. Many players think they are serving low, but their serves actually cross the net too high and bounce too high. Or they think they are serving heavy backspin but aren't getting enough spin Or they don't vary their backspin serves with no-spin serves.

Second, you challenge him by varying the spin and placement, and mixing in long serves.

Third, you can serve from the middle or forehand side of the table so you have an angle into the short forehand, and then vary between serving short to the forehand and long to the backhand, using the same motion. (It's most effective if you can serve short to the forehand with a backhand sidespin type serve.)

Ultimately, you cannot stop a receiver from trying to attack your serves, but you can maximize the number of mistakes he'll make in doing so. If he makes too many, either you win from that, or he'll have to reconsider his aggressive receives.

June 1, 2015 – Fast No-Spin Serves to the Middle

Free Points – who wants 'em?!!! Oh, you, the reader? Well then, here's the *easiest* way to get a free point in table tennis – a fast no-spin serve to the middle. (That's usually the opponent's elbow, the transition point between forehand and backhand, though it varies for some players.) Here is what often happens when you do this:

- Because it comes to the middle, the receiver has to make a snap decision on whether to use forehand or backhand.
- The receiver then has to move quickly against a fast incoming ball, often after a slow start as he decided between forehand and backhand.
- Because it comes fast, the receiver is rushed and has little time to make these decisions and movements.
- Because the receiver has little time to make these decisions and movements, he tends to shorten his stroke and lose some control.
- Because it has no spin, the ball tends to "die" when it contacts the opponent's racket.

- Because the receiver tends to shorten his stroke and lose some control, he isn't able to generate the extra force needed to lift the no-spin ball, nor does he have the control to get the proper racket angle, and so the ball dies and goes into the net.
- Because the ball is coming fast, and most fast serves have topspin, the receiver tends to receive it like a topspin, and so goes into the net.

Even when this serve is read properly, most players are forced to take the serve late and lift it, often setting the server up for an easy attack. But unless overused, many receivers will struggle with this over and over. If used two or three times a game, this is a free point about half the time against players rated under 2000, and it can be pretty effective against stronger players as well. It is especially effective against your normal two-winged player, who is ready to receive forehand or backhand. It is a bit less effective against a one-winged looper with fast footwork, who will usually loop the serve, but against that type of player you change and serve fast no-spin to the wide corners.

How do you do the serve? First, learn a basic fast topspin serve. Contact the ball perhaps a foot behind the end-line, as low to the table as possible (below net height), with some topspin. Hit it so it lands as close to your own end-line as possible; this maximizes how much table you'll have for the ball to drop on the far side. By serving crosscourt you'll be able to serve faster, but you should also learn to serve it down the line and of course to the middle. If the ball hits near your end-line, crosses the net low, but doesn't bounce within about six inches of the opponent's end-line, then you haven't maximized your speed.

Put bottles or other targets on the far end of the table, right at the edge – one on each corner, and two where the opponents' playing elbows would be. (One for a righty, one for a lefty.) Then practice serving fast and knocking them off. Until you can do this pretty consistently, you aren't really controlling your serve. Use targets that won't fall over or you'll have to constantly pick them up. (But it's sometimes fun to use paper cups and see how easily you can knock them off the table.)

Now you're ready for the real point-winner – a fast no-spin to the elbow. There's only one difference between this and a regular fast topspin serve: at contact, instead of putting topspin on the ball, you hit the ball with a very slight downward motion. Don't think heavy backspin; it's more of a glancing downward blow to put a little backspin on the ball. If you serve no-spin, after two bounces on the table the ball has some topspin. To truly deaden it, you need a little backspin at the start.

Now work on speed. Because you won't have topspin to pull the ball down, you won't be able to serve a no-spin (or slight backspin) quite as fast as with topspin, but you can still serve it very fast. It just takes practice. Put the target where the opponent's elbow would be, and practice hitting it as fast as you can. If you have trouble generating speed, stop trying to serve on the table and just serve as fast as you can. Then gradually work on getting the ball to hit the table, slowing down the serve only as much as necessary.

The fast no-spin serve to the middle is not nearly as hard to learn as it might sound. You just have to put in a few hours of practice. And once learned, you'll have it for the rest of your table tennis life – and the number of free points you'll get from this serve over a lifetime will dwarf the time you spent on learning it.

June 30, 2014 – Forehand or Backhand Serve & Attack

If you want to reach a high level in table tennis, it's pretty much a given that you need to serve and attack. There are many ways of doing this; it's just a matter of finding ways that match your game. At the higher levels, it's almost all serve and loop, though others serve and hit. You can serve backspin and loop against the likely pushed return, or you can serve topspin and loop or hit the likely countered or topspinned return.

Should you try to serve and attack with your forehand? Or should you attack with your backhand? That's a question every aspiring player needs to address. And the answer is yes and no.

In general, the forehand attack is more powerful. Therefore, when possible, most players should look to follow their serves up with their forehand. Players who are very fast on their feet and with very good forehands might even force it, running around their backhands to play forehands nearly every time the serve is returned there (at least if it's deep enough to loop). Players who aren't as fast should still look for chances to follow up with the forehand, especially off weak returns off the serve that can be put away.

But even if you can follow the serve up with a forehand, should you do so every time? Probably not. A forehand from the backhand side puts you out of position, and so allows your opponent to block or counter-attack to your wide forehand. You may be fast enough to get to that ball, but it's going to wear you down, and even if you make the shot, it leaves you open on the backhand side. Plus, to cover that wide forehand, you probably have to move immediately after the first forehand, meaning you'll likely be open on your backhand side if the opponent returns the first ball there. The more you attack from the backhand side with your forehand, the more your opponent can get into a rhythm off your attacks, and so he'll get more and more consistent at it.

So rather than become predictable and allowing your opponent to get into a rhythm, mix in some serve and backhand attacks. If your opponent pushes long to your backhand, backhand loop. If you serve topspin and he counters or topspins to your backhand, drive or loop with the backhand. Don't let him get into that rhythm where he knows what you are going to do before you do it. Make him adjust to both forehand and backhand attacks – the shots come out differently, and can cause havoc if you mix them up.

There are advantages to backhand attacks. Besides staying in position, you are facing the opponent as you hit or loop the shot, so you can see what he's doing and where he's positioned right up until the instant you are committed to your own shot. This allows you to more accurately go after his middle (transition between backhand and forehand, usually around the playing elbow), or to switch to a wide angle if you see him out of position. Also, backhand attacks are often quicker and with a shorter stroke, and so will cause timing problems for the opponent, especially if you go back and forth between forehand and backhand attacks. Even the spins are different; most players get more topspin from one side or the other. (A surprising number of players get more spin on their backhand loops than their forehand, causing a lot of balls to be blocked off the end.)

Another consideration is your own serve. If you serve heavy backspin, you are likely to get a heavy push return to the backhand. There's often no huge advantage to looping this with the forehand, so you might as well backhand loop. On the other hand, if you serve with more sidespin or no-spin, and your opponent still pushes it, it's likely to have less backspin and likely pop up a bit. So for those serves you might want to favor the forehand so you can more easily put the ball away.

So develop both a serve and forehand attack and serve and backhand attack. Two guns are better than one.

RALLYING TACTICS

April 7, 2014 – Attacking the Middle

The middle is the weakest spot for most players. When I say middle, I don't mean the middle of the table; it's the mid-point between the opponent's forehand and backhand, usually where the playing elbow is. Most beginning players play to the opponent's forehand or backhand, while most intermediate players play wider angles. Advanced players know that while angled attacks are good, the best place for the first attack (and often follow-up attacks) is right at the middle.

Why is the middle so weak when attacked? There are five (yes, *five!*) primary reasons.

1. The player has to make a decision on whether to play forehand or backhand, and often hesitates. When the ball goes to the forehand or backhand there is no such decision to make.

2. The player has to move in an uncomfortable direction. Most players find moving wide to cover the forehand or backhand an easier move since you are moving into the shot. Covering the middle means essentially getting out of the way of the ball, which is usually a more difficult move.

3. When you attack the middle, it forces your opponent to move out of position to cover it. This opens up the corners. One of the best one-two combos is an attack to the middle followed by an angled attack. Or you can go to the middle a second or third time as your opponent struggles to cover it.

4. Attacking the middle takes away the extreme angles for your opponent. If you attack a wide corner, your opponent can return at an equally wide angle.

5. Players don't get much practice covering the middle, both because opponents don't give them this shot much until the higher levels, and because most don't practice against it.

Attacking the middle isn't just an option; it should be the default place to attack unless you have a reason to go elsewhere, such as an open corner, a slow opponent who doesn't cover the corners well, or an opponent who is weaker on one side. The nice thing about attacking the middle is that even if the opponent knows it's coming he can't really prepare for it. If he tries to favor one side to cover it, you simply move your target over to compensate.

While you should usually be aggressive when going to the middle, there are at least two other times you might go to the middle with a less aggressive shot. First, against a two-winged attacker, you might serve or push deep to the middle to make him decide whether to forehand or backhand attack and then move to do so. Second, going to the middle cuts off the angles, so a passive shot can't be attacked at a wide angle. (But a smart opponent might instead attack your middle!)

Why don't players attack the middle more often? There are two primary reasons. First, it's difficult to hit because it's a moving target. When you attack the wide forehand or wide backhand, it's the same place no matter who you play. But the middle changes not only from player to player but throughout the rally against the same opponent, depending on where he is standing and what he is looking to do. (An example of the latter is if the opponent is looking to attack with his forehand, then going to his middle only gives him an easier forehand, so his "middle" moves toward his backhand side.) The only way to develop the ability to attack this moving target is by doing it over and over in matches and drills until it becomes second nature. And this leads to the second reason players don't attack the middle more often: because they don't *practice* attacking the middle.

Most players practice their attacks either crosscourt or down the line to their partner's block, and so they go to the partner's forehand or backhand, over and over. This becomes a habit. If all one does is attack to the forehand or backhand in practice, how likely is the player going to go to the middle in a match? You have to practice it if you want to do it in a match. Here are some drills you can do to practice attacking the middle.

1. **Attack the Middle Drill.** Have your practice partner stand in a neutral position so you can see where his middle is. Then drill into that spot, either looping or hitting. Your practice partner moves over and blocks, either all forehand or all backhand. However, there are two variations to this. Your partner can also block with either all backhand or forehand, but move back to a neutral position after each shot, so he can practice moving to cover the middle. A third way, the most difficult, is he stands in a neutral position and blocks back either forehand or backhand.

2. **Serve and Attack Middle Drill.** You serve backspin, your partner pushes back (either to a pre-arranged spot or random), and you attack his middle. Then play out the point.

3. **Practice Matches.** Play practice matches where your first attack goes to the middle every time.

So learn to attack the middle, and soon you'll leave the middle of the pack as you move up the ladder of table tennis success!

November 28, 2016 – Follow the Elbow

Many players are aware that one of the best places to attack is an opponent's middle, i.e. his playing elbow, roughly the mid-point between forehand and backhand. There are multiple reasons for this [as noted in the preceding Tip, "Attacking the Middle"]. Many make the mistake of looking for a chance to attack the middle instead of just attacking it, period. Why wait?

Often a player is told to attack the opponent's middle to set up shots to the corners. This is a highly effective tactic, but unless you do it regularly, it's actually difficult to do correctly. The problem is that after attacking the middle, one of the corners usually opens up – but then you have to almost instantly judge which one that is. If you get it wrong, the opponent often gets an easy shot. Top players are so used to attacking the middle and then going to the corner that opens up that it's instinct – they find it so easily they don't even realize how difficult this is for others.

How do you judge which side opens up? In covering the middle, the opponent has to move sideways to play a forehand or backhand from the middle. That leaves one side open. After the shot, they are usually either slow in returning into position, thereby leaving that side open, or almost as often move too quickly, often still moving as you hit your next shot, and so leave the other side open. You just have to see and react to which side is open.

But there's a simpler tactic which anyone can do which is just about as effective and is easier to do – and that's to simply keep going after the middle, i.e. "Follow the Elbow." This is an especially good tactic in fast exchanges, especially backhand ones. All you do is keep punching or looping the ball right at the opponent's elbow, no matter where they are. If they start edging over to cover it, you follow the target and keep going after it. The tactic isn't too effective against super-fast forehand players, but most players are two-winged in fast rallies. Even if they know you are going to go to their middle again, they can't really position themselves for it – all that does is move their elbow, and you simply go for it again.

Against such an onslaught to their elbow, many players will just wilt, unable to rally effectively. Have no mercy – keep going at their elbow until they either miss or give you an easy put-away – and then you can go anywhere.

March 2, 2015 – When Should You Go for a Winner?

All players need good put-away shots, whether it be forehand or backhand loops or smashes. But when should you use them? Here are four theories on this.

1. When the ball is high. Patiently work until you get that high ball, and don't get impatient and go for a crazy shot.
2. When the ball lands toward the middle of the table, depth-wise. These are often easy to put away or at least attack strongly. It's why coaches stress keeping the ball mostly short at the start of a point (by serving or pushing short) and mostly deep once the rally begins. Most soft topspin and backspin shots that don't go deep but don't die over the table (i.e. backspin balls that would bounce twice given the chance) should at least be attacked pretty hard, and by the advanced intermediate level they should be consistently put away.

104

3. The 51% Ogimura Doctrine – if you have a 51% chance of making your put-away (assuming your opponent can't return it), you go for it. If he may return it, you need a higher percentage.
4. Flashbulb Theory of Larry (FTL). With experience, there'll come times when a little flashbulb goes off in your head that tells you that you have read the ball perfectly and are in perfect position. The ball might be low and deep, and ripping it might be seemingly difficult, but if that flashbulb goes off, then you should probably take the shot. In fact, not taking the shot could throw you off due to indecision. Of course, the key here is having an accurate flashbulb that only goes off when you really have read the ball and are set to take the shot – and that takes experience. And even when that flashbulb goes off, you don't have to hit the ball faster than light, just hard enough to win the point.

September 7, 2015 – Never Look for a Winner

Many players are always looking for shots to put away, especially when serving. The problem here is that if you consciously look for shots to put away, then you are consciously taking control of your shots instead of letting your training (i.e. your subconscious) do what it's been trained to do. Instead, just let the shots happen, i.e. let your trained reflexes take over.

If there's a shot you can put away, your training should take over and you'll put the ball away. If it's not a shot you can put away, then your training will allow you to react appropriately – but if you were consciously looking for a ball to put away, then that won't happen as you've put aside your training to consciously take control. If your training *doesn't* take control properly, then you need to train yourself so that it *does* happen.

How do you train yourself to reflexively go for winners when the shot is there? Practice. (Pause, while you stop groaning.) And how do you do that? Here are two ways.

- With a coach: He can feed you multiball where he mixes in difficult and easy shots, and you put away the easy ones. After each shot is when you consciously think about whether you went for the right shot. You can do this against either backspin or topspin, or a mixture.

- With a practice partner or coach, or in practice matches: Practice your serve and attack, where you have to judge each time if your partner's return can be put away or not. Try to clear your mind and let your reactions take over. It is after each rally that you should consciously think about whether you went for the right shot. If you think about it, your subconscious will get the message.

When should you go for a put-away shot? That's different for everyone, but you'll learn when to do it with experience and practice. Obviously high balls should be put away, but you should also learn to put away most balls that land in the middle of the table (depth-wise), shots where you aren't rushed or pressured (by the ball's speed, spin, or placement), and perhaps even off a strong shot when you read and time the ball just right.

November 10, 2014 – Keep the Ball Deep

One of the most important things that distinguish top players from others is the depth of their shots. There are times when you want to keep the ball short on the table – short serves and pushes (to stop opponents from looping), short blocks (as a change of pace), and wide-angle shots (allowing you to go outside the corners for extreme angles). Counterloops often don't go deep on the table – it's hard to control depth from way off the table. However, these are the exceptions. In most cases you want most of your shots to go deep on the table – pushes, blocks, counterhits, drives, loops, chops, fishes, and lobs. You also want your deep serves to go truly deep.

By going deep you give yourself time to react to the opponent's shot. You take away the extreme angles, and so have less table to cover. Finally, balls that land in the middle of the table (depth-wise) are easier to attack. Most intermediate players can loop kill or smash them, and advanced players rip these balls with ease. By going deep you make it difficult for your opponent to hit winners or even to play aggressively.

When you see advanced players returning shot after shot, usually it's not that they have incredible reflexes; it's that they are keeping the ball deep, and so can react to the opponent's shots. Weaker players usually put their shots shorter and are unable to react to their opponent's shots, and then they mistakenly blame it on slower reflexes. (Advanced players also place the ball well, often to wide corners, forcing the opponent to move.)

How does one go about learning depth control?

First, be aware of the depth of your shots. If I catch a ball in the middle of a rally and ask my opponent where his last shot was, he'll usually know the direction but will often have no clue about the depth. Depth awareness often doesn't really come about for many players until they approach the advanced levels – and this lack of awareness often stops players from reaching those levels.

Second, strive to keep the ball deep on most shots, both in games and practice. Stop playing safe, middle-of-the-table shots that are effective against weaker players but are easy balls to attack for stronger ones. Aim for the last 18 inches or so of the table, and you'll develop the habit of keeping the ball deep – and the average level of your opponents' shots will go down dramatically. (Keep in mind that the goal isn't to hit the ball 18 inches from the end-line; it's to hit the ball *within* 18 inches of the end-line. So your average shot might actually be within a foot of the end-line.)

Third, practice your depth shots. Once they are past the beginning levels most players stop thinking about simple drills like forehand to forehand and backhand to backhand – but it is simple drills like these where you can learn depth control. Put a string or some other marker across the table, about 18 inches from the end-line, and see if you consistently keep the ball past it. Don't try to consciously guide the shot; learn the feel for keeping the ball deep, and let your subconscious take over, just as it should for all learned shots. Perhaps have one player block while the other attacks, and both try to keep the ball deep.

You can practice this on your own with a box of balls. Bounce them on your side of the table and hit to the far side with various shots, and learn the feel for keeping the ball deep. You can practice depth on pushes, drives, and loops in this way. Perhaps put a box against the end-line on the far side and see if you can fill the box up with balls. It's not exactly the same as hitting against an incoming ball, but it's close enough to practice getting the feel for depth.

You should similarly practice the depth on your long serves. If your serve isn't supposed to go short (so given the chance the second bounce would be on the table or at most barely long – a "half-long" serve), then you want the first bounce to be very deep, within 6-12 inches of the end-line. You have complete control of your serves, so you should have even greater depth control with them than with rallying shots.

Keep the ball deep and your level will leap!

February 3, 2014 – Winning with Ball Control

If you cannot match up with your opponent using speed or spin, then you need other weapons. One of the best ways to beat faster and more powerful players ("bashers") is with ball control. Just as an all-out attacker uses his serve and receive to set up his attack, a ball control player uses serve and receive to take control of the rally. For him, it's all about ball control, placement, and shot selection. If he's able to use his ball control to make the basher uncomfortable, he's won the battle. So how do you do this?

Start with receive, for it is while serving that bashers dominate, given the chance. But is he really dominating on his own, or are you letting him dominate? For example, if the basher has a strong forehand, and follows his serve with his forehand over and over, what are you doing to stop this? Few players can really dominate the whole table with the forehand against well-placed shots. Does the basher really do so, or is the receiver keeping the ball well inside the corners, so the basher doesn't have to cover the whole table? Ball control means ball control; the ball control player needs to be able to return the serve anywhere on the table. This means mostly one of two things: either pinning the basher down by relentlessly returning the ball to the extreme wide backhand (even outside the corner if returning crosscourt), or by aiming it there and last-second returning it to the extreme wide forehand (again, even outside the corner for crosscourt shots). If you can't do this, then you don't have the ball control (yet) to play a ball control game. How can you learn to do so? By practicing it in game after game until you get it down.

Now suppose your opponent attacks off his serve from both wings, so wide-angled returns to the backhand aren't really effective. Now the basher is ready to bash from both wings – or is he? Try quick returns to his elbow (or a little to his backhand if he favors the forehand from the middle), and watch his shots begin to crumble as he makes last-second decisions. Plus, by going to the middle, it draws the basher out of position, giving you an opening to the corners on the next shot.

Now we move on to serving. The basher serves so he can attack, usually trying to end the point as quickly as possible. The ball control player should also mostly serve so he can attack, but in his case he's not trying to end the point quickly. He's looking to attack to make the basher uncomfortable, because the basher isn't comfortable when he's not attacking. So attack first, and force him to either defend or go for difficult counterattacks. The key again is placement. Go to the side that gives the attacker the most trouble. If he can't block or counterloop consistently on the forehand, then nail him there over and over. Even if he does make the return – even a strong one – it opens him up on the backhand side. Or attack his middle (roughly his elbow), which should be your default opening attack anyway. Or if he's weak on the backhand defense (usually blocking), then go there. Or drive him crazy by going everywhere. Just do each shot with a purpose – to make the basher uncomfortable, and to take him out of position for the next shot.

Once in the rally, the ball control player has a 2-1 advantage over the basher. He wins most of the points when he has the initiative, as does the attacker. But when neither has the initiative, guess who has the advantage? The ball control player, who has successfully taken away the basher's attack, thereby bringing him down a level.

January 26, 2015 – Play the Ball

Often players ask me how to play different surfaces. There are obvious and easy answers for that, and beginners do need to know how the various surfaces play different. For example, long pips tends to return whatever spin you give it, and they need to understand that to be able to play it. Short pips tends to return flatter (i.e. less spinny) then you'd expect from the more common inverted. And so on.

But the more important thing is to simply learn to play the ball. You don't really need to know that long pips will return your spin, except perhaps as a help at the start of a match. Very early in any match you'll see how your opponent's surfaces and strokes return your shots, and that's what you need to play. For example, knowing that long pips will return your spin is fine, but some types return more than others, and some strokes with long pips return more than others. Players need to match what actually is happening in a match to how they react, not just memorize something they can read in a book.

The same is true of adjusting to an opponent's strokes. If he does something strange, ignore the strangeness and just adjust to playing the balls he's giving you. (And remember that if a player has strange shots, then there's a reason they are strange shots – they are not orthodox, and so likely have major technical weaknesses in them, if you can find them.)

Once a player understands how the ball comes off an opponent's racket and strokes in a match, he can play the balls he's getting, knowing that they'll be based on how they have been coming off the racket so far. Then he can figure out how to adjust, and what type of shots he should do to get the type of balls he wants. For example, you might have trouble against the fast dead shots of a pips-out player. But then you'll realize that you have to contact the ball differently, perhaps lifting slightly more with more topspin (assuming you are a topspin player), and even noting that if you keep the ball deep, you have more time to react and adjust to these deader balls. You could read that in a book or article, but it'll sink in a lot better when you actually face such a situation and adjust, learn to play the ball your opponent is giving you, and actually make the adjustment and win!

PLAYING SPECIFIC STYLES

February 16, 2015 – Playing Off-Table Two-Winged Topspinners
Some players like to step off the table and just topspin away, turning many opponents into blockers who are jammed at the table, unable to do anything other than struggle to keep the ball in play. These topspinners can seemingly go on forever, and eventually either outlast or wear out the blocker, or find an easy ball to loop away. At higher levels, such players are often overpowered, as it's the very nature of their game that the opponent can take the attack – but it takes a certain level of strokes and footwork to do this consistently. And often this is exactly what the off-table topspinner wants his opponent to do, to try to overpower him, and thereby make mistakes.

So how does one beat such a player? Here are some standard tactics.

1. **Bring him in and then attack.** Do this with short serves and short receives, and then catch him too close to the table with your first attack, before he can get into his comfortable, off-table pocket. Since these players hang off the table, attacking their serve often plays right into their game. You don't have to win the point on the first attack after bringing them in; it's sufficient to force a weak return that you can follow up with a winner.

2. **Get your forehand into play.** Because he plays off the table, you have more time to get your forehand into position, rather than just block. You might have to take a half step off the table to give yourself time. (Many players get stuck blocking because they are too jammed at the table, and so don't have time to do more than block.) It's important that you punish the opponent for his soft play by attacking, and especially being ready to attack when you get a weak return, in particular balls that land short. When the ball does land short, blast a winner to a wide angle or right at the opponent's playing elbow (midway between forehand and backhand). (If your forehand is so weak that you cannot attack these soft topspins when you are in position, then you need to work on your forehand attack.)

3. **Mostly attack the middle and wide backhand.** Generally avoid the forehand, where most off-table topspinners have more range, get more spin, and have better counter-attacks. (So generally, when going after the middle, perhaps aim it *slightly* toward the backhand side.) But it depends on the player. Some off-table topspinners are more vulnerable on the forehand side. Unless he's simply a much better player, he's unlikely to beat you in a duel between his off-table backhand, where he has to cover both his wide backhand and middle, against your forehand looping or smashing, assuming you don't try to overpower him on one shot. Players like this often seem open to the wide corners, but in reality they usually cover that area pretty well. So make sure to go to both the wide backhand and middle, and perhaps the wide forehand, depending on the player. (This was

one of the reasons Ilija Lupulesku – a Yugoslavian/Serbian/USA star who played an off-table two-winged looping/fishing/lobbing game – was so successful for years despite backing off the table so much, since players relentlessly went after his wide backhand and didn't go after his middle nearly enough.)

4. **Change the pace.** Do this with either soft loops or soft blocks. Find out early which side he's more vulnerable to a change of pace, but it's usually on the forehand side. This is where a chop or sidespin block can be valuable. He'll likely make a weak return that you can attack, often catching him too close to the table or throwing off his timing. If an opponent gets into a rhythm where he's getting everything back, it's imperative that you change the pace to throw off that rhythm.

5. **Be patient.** Your goal isn't to blast a winner every shot; your goal is to play for an easy ball to blast for a winner, usually a ball that lands short that you can blast to a wide corner or right at his middle.

June 2, 2014 – Playing Short pips

Short pips dominated the 1960s and much of the 1970s. (They are often called pips-out, which can be confusing as long pips is also pips-out, though conventionally speaking pips-out means short pips.) But by the 1990s inverted was pretty much dominating. The last great short pips player was probably Liu Guoliang, the 1996 Olympic Gold Medalist for Men's Singles and the 1999 World Men's Singles Champion. But as two-winged loopers became more and more powerful while playing closer to the table, and with the ball going from 38mm to 40mm in 2000 (which slowed the game down some, a disadvantage for most short pips players) the day of the short pips player pretty much died – there are very few left at the elite levels. At the club level, the style is also dying out as the huge majority of players use inverted.

But one of the ironies of this is that since there are fewer short-pips players, inverted players often no longer know how to play them. And so the time is ripe for short pips players to dominate again – at least at the intermediate level, where players not only don't know how to play them, but don't yet have the powerful and consistent looping games of the elite.

I had great difficulty my first few years against short-pips players, but I played against several of them regularly – and then they became one of the easiest surfaces for me to play against. Since I'm used to playing them and know how to do so, I'd rather play a short pips player now than an inverted one any day – you've got a gun and he's using a bow and arrow. (But beware – some of these short pips players are still deadly with their bow and arrow!)

So how do you play a short-pips player? This is sort of like asking how to play an inverted player; there are many styles of short pips players. But here are some general tips that will work against nearly all short pips players.

1. Keep the ball deep on the table. This both makes things difficult for the short pips player, but also gives you more time to react to a ball that you aren't as used to. Against a deep ball he can't rush you, nor can he create heavy spin.

2. Don't take on a short pips player in a battle of quickness. Find your comfort zone, as close to the table as you are comfortable and consistent. When in trouble (especially if rushed), back up and spin the ball deep on the table.

3. Remember that their blocks and hits are deader than you expect since you are used to playing inverted, so if you don't adjust by aiming your loops and drives slightly higher, you'll go into the net. Because the ball is dead, you'll have to use a bit more force to generate the same amount of topspin. (An incoming topspin ball rebounds out with topspin, while you can convert the spin of an incoming backspin ball into topspin. You can't do either with a dead ball.) One problem you'll have to overcome is many short pips players will rush you, and so you have less time to stroke, and yet you may need a longer stroke to generate topspin if you are looping. Or just go with a bit less spin, but control the ball deep on the table.

4. If you keep looping into the net, don't think of the short pips block as a block; think of it as a very quick push without that much spin.

5. Surprisingly, many players have the opposite problem when looping against a short-pips blocker – they loop off the end. This is because they are rushed, and when rushed, most players over-react and lift too much. Perhaps more importantly, they back off the table expecting the ball to jump out to them (as an inverted ball would), and so by the time the ball gets to them, it's dropping, and so the looper has to adjust and lift a ball that's dropping – and they often over-react by over-lifting, and go off the end.

6. Remember that their serves and pushes have less spin than you are used to. The real problem here is that if you are used to playing inverted players, your instinctive reaction is off, as you'll reflexively expect more spin. The only cure is to play against them, and learn to adjust.

7. Most importantly, play against short pips players every chance you can, and you'll become comfortable against them and soon realize why short pips has almost died out at the higher levels. They are easy to play against once you are used to playing them. They cannot put as much spin on the ball, so short pips serves, pushes, and loops (which they can do against backspin) are less spinny, which is a weakness when you get used to it. They don't have as much topspin to pull the ball down, and so have difficulty against deep and spinny topspins and backspin. Because short pips doesn't rebound the ball out as easily as inverted, short pips players have to stroke the ball more when blocking and hitting, and so they are weaker when they have to move, especially in covering the middle, so attack there every chance. Ultimately, a good looper can turn most short pips players into blockers, and in the modern game, winning by blocking is more and more difficult than by looping. (But there are still some very good blockers out there.)

January 20, 2014 – Playing Against the Seemiller or American Grip
(This is an excerpt from "Table Tennis Tactics for Thinkers.")
This grip was named for and popularized by five-time U.S. Men's Singles Champion Dan Seemiller, who was ranked in the top thirty in the

world in the late 1970s. He was followed by Eric Boggan, who reached top twenty in the world. No other U.S.-trained player has come close to these rankings in the sponge era (since the 1950s). Four of the five U.S. team members at the 1983 World Championships used this grip – Dan Seemiller, his brother Rick Seemiller, Eric Boggan, and 1983 Pan Am Men's Singles Gold Medalist Brian Masters. (All four are in the U.S. Table Tennis Hall of Fame.) The grip is sometimes called the American grip, but is more commonly called the Seemiller grip.

The grip is sort of a variation of the shakehands grip, with the top of the racket rotated to the left so that the index finger curls around the side of the racket. The forehand is played about the same, but on the backhand the arm rotates about so that the same side is used on the forehand and backhand. Despite its promising start, the grip never came close to the popularity of shakehands or penhold, and in recent years fewer and fewer players use the grip. However, you will face these players in tournaments (especially in the northeast U.S.) and need to be ready.

Like shakehands and penhold, the Seemiller grip also has its backhand and forehand variations, except here it is more extreme. If the top of the racket is rotated to the left, it is a backhand grip, as used by Eric Boggan and Brian Masters, which weakens the forehand loop. If the racket is rotated to the right (almost becoming a regular shakehands grip), it is a forehand grip, as used by Dan and Rick Seemiller, which weakens the backhand.

The Seemiller grip has four major advantages. It is probably the best grip for blocking, especially on the backhand. There is very little weakness in the middle – in fact, the grip is at its best there. It gives a very natural wrist snap on forehand loops against backspin. And since only one side of the racket is used, and because the racket is easy to flip with this grip, it allows a player to have an off-surface on selected shots, usually antispin, though some use long pips. A player with this grip can flip to use that side as a variation, and then flip back to the regular surface, usually inverted. (All four of the U.S. team members mentioned above used antispin on the reverse side, inverted on the other.)

The disadvantages are that the wrist can make it difficult to play the corners (and so players with this grip often have trouble with players who play to the wide corners); it limits the backhand mostly to close-to-the-table blocking and hitting, with a very limited backhand loop; and it can be difficult to counterloop with this grip.

Because of the lack of a strong backhand loop, deep serves and pushes to the backhand can give this grip problems, unless the player has very fast footwork and can play the forehand from the backhand over and over. (Others, like Eric Boggan, learned to hit backspin serves with his antispin side, and then flipped back to inverted for the next shot.)

Some players with the Seemiller grip can be absolute walls on the backhand, and it makes no sense trying to overpower that side – but if you attack the forehand side first (and perhaps force them to step off the table) and then come back to the backhand, then the backhand wall might crumble. The grip is weaker from off the table, and like most shots, is less consistent when you have to move.

Most players with the Seemiller grip use the off surface to return serves, especially short ones. Some have the ability to quickly judge the depth of the incoming serve, and use anti against short serves, inverted to loop or otherwise attack long serves. If they use the anti to return most serves, serve deep, and you should get a relatively weak return or an erratic anti attack. Often a deep serve to the forehand is especially effective. If they try to flip the racket based on the depth of your serve, mix in short spinny serves and fast, long serves, and watch them struggle to flip their racket appropriately – it's not easy! It is very important not to telegraph your serves – players like this are very good at picking up small cues, so try to use the exact same motion for both short and long serves, at least until contact.

PLAYING WITH OR AGAINST A COACH

September 26, 2016 – How to Play Against a Player with a Coach

Imagine playing a tournament match. It's you versus your opponent in this gladiatorial combat, with both players alone out there, on their own. Except . . . that's not what happen when your opponent has a coach. It's no longer you versus your opponent, it's two against one, and you are the one. How can you best handle this? Here are some tips.

1. **Ignore the coach.** If you let it get into your head and bother you, that will likely hurt you more than any golden words of advice the coach might say.

2. **Get your own coach.** It evens the playing field, both tactically and psychologically. Often all you need is a sounding board between games, and even the appearance of having a coach can affect the opponent.

3. **Take advantage of it psychologically.** You are thinking for yourself, while your opponent isn't. This should give you confidence. Most of the time your opponent is out there alone, just like you. While he's thinking, "What did my coach tell me to do?", you are thinking, "What should I do tactically?" You have the superior thinking pattern here as you are thinking for yourself, and better able to adjust to changes in the game.

4. **Watch what your opponent does at the start of a new game and adjust.** You figured out what your opponent is doing on your own; will your opponent be able to adjust to you without his coach?

5. **Play differently at the start of a new game.** If you do this, your opponent, often a kid (or adult) who's just been told how to play against what you did in the *previous* game, will likely fall apart in frustration, since the tactics he was just given no longer work. You can literally alternate tactics each game. It's one of the reasons it's important to have a "B" game. This is probably the most important tactic when playing a player with a coach. Here's an actual example of how I used this in a tournament match.

    In the first game, I mostly served backspin and looped his pushes. On his serve, I mostly forced rallies, often backhand-to-backhand, and out-steadied him. I won the game, but it was relatively close – the opponent was rated lower than me, but was competitive. I knew his coach would tell him to quick-push my serves to wide corners to stop my forehand attack, and to attack my middle in rallies. So in the second game I switched to serving mostly short side-top and no-spin serves (all disguised as backspin) that he proceeded to quick-push ten feet off the table. In rallies I went on the forehand attack and feasted on his balls to my middle. He got very frustrated and I won the second easily. In the third I went back to my first-game tactics and won all the points at the start. The coach called a timeout, but when they returned I switched to my second-game tactics, and went up 10-0. (I played a lobbing point there and sort of gave him a point, and then won 11-1.) After the match the poor kid threw a tantrum, blaming his coach for the loss.

So next time you play a match against someone with a coach, take advantage of the situation!

December 28, 2016 – Coaching and Playing Under the New ITTF Coaching Rule

As of Oct. 1, 2016, the ITTF changed the coaching rule. Before that time, coaching was allowed only between games and timeouts. Now the rule is, "Players may receive advice at any time except during rallies provided play is not thereby delayed."

What does this mean for players and coaches? In theory, it means coaches can tell players what to do every point, either by calling it out (perhaps in a language the opposing player or coach does not know) or signaling. It means a player can look back before each serve and the coach can signal what serve to use. It means that when a coach sees the player is doing something tactically wrong, he can tell the player immediately, rather than waiting until the end of the game or calling a one-time timeout.

In practice, it's not that simple. In most cases, calling out advice is risky as the opponent (or coach or friend of the player nearby) may know the language. In many cases, the coach might only know one language, and is so handicapped. So this type of coaching will mostly take place when a ball happens to come by the barrier where the coach is, and the coach can then whisper something to the player. This can, of course, be abused – a player may take a sudden walk around the court, getting close enough to the coach to hear his whispered advice, and will likely get away with it. (But woe be the player who is too transparent, and, say, kicks the ball toward his coach so he can go pick it up!)

In reality, except for the serve, table tennis is a game of reacting to an opponent, and trying to over-coach often turns a player from reacting to the opponent to over-anticipating (and thereby *not* reacting properly to the opponent). So coaches and players should be very careful about coaching during a game on most areas.

However, the serve is different. I expect that more and more coaches and players will set up signals whereby the coach can signal in serves. Some coaches will want to do so every serve. I think that's a mistake, as it turns the player into essentially a mindless zombie. Instead, coaches will likely develop signals to emphasize what serves the player should *favor*. For example, if a player keeps serving deep, and the coach wants him to serve short, he doesn't need to signal every serve; he simply needs a signal that says "serve short more." Or one for "serve long more." Or "more backspin serves." And so on.

That doesn't mean the coach won't want to signal (or whisper) other advise, but only sparingly. If a player is, say, playing too much to the backhand, the coach doesn't need to signal each point for him to play more to the forehand or middle; he needs a general signal for this to remind the player.

The problem with a player receiving constant coaching during a game is that he will tend to stop thinking for himself, and so will always have to rely on the coach. You can't learn to think tactically unless you are thinking tactically, and so a player who relies too much on the coach will grow up to be weak tactically. On the other hand, a player who learns to think for himself, but gets periodic signals – "corrections" – from a coach, can learn to think for himself, especially as he learns to self-correct and learn why the coach wants him to make certain tactical changes.

One practical concern is which side of the table the player is on. If the player is on his side, the coach can often whisper advice to him. When he's on the far side, the coach can signal to him (with the opposing player's back to him).

So what should a player with a match coach do? Before the match, work out signals with the coach. Keep them simple; if you spend your time trying to remember what each signal means, it means you won't be thinking about what you should be thinking about, i.e. tactical thinking. Perhaps a signal about short or long serves (including fast ones, such as down the line); type of serve (forehand pendulum, backhand serve, etc.); service spin (backspin, topspin, sidespin, no-spin); placement (forehand, backhand, middle); and for playing more (or less) aggressive. These are some of the common things that coaches might want to communicate to a player in a match. But overuse of even service signals will probably be counter-productive – instead, the player should be making these decisions, with the coach giving occasional input when he thinks a major change is needed.

CHAPTER SIX: IMPROVING

GENERAL

August 4, 2014 – How to Move Up a Level

What does it mean to move up a level in table tennis? I'd define two players to be on different levels if it would be a major upset if one defeated the other. Another way of looking at it would be to say that if the stronger player plays his normal level, he would win pretty much every time. Based on this, I'd say a level in table tennis ranges from about 300 points at the lower levels (under 1000 or so), to about 50-100 points at the higher levels (over 2500 or so). For most USATT members, a level would be about 100-200 rating points.

How can you move up a level in table tennis? It means improving all parts of your game, as a weakness in your game is like a weak link in a chain.

You could work hard, dramatically improve one aspect of your game, and hope to move up a level. But it's not that simple. Suppose you develop a really nice forehand loop. With this weapon, you would think that your level would go up dramatically. And sure enough, you will do better against players around your own level. But when you play players a level higher, their level is far enough ahead of yours that they'll simply do something to disarm your new weapon. They may serve short, push short, push very heavy, throw spinny or fast serves at you, use ball placement, block well, force backhand exchanges, play quick shots so you don't have time to loop, or simply attack first. In each case, they'll take your weapon away from you, and you still won't move up that coveted level. Often, a stronger player will seem to win on one of his strengths, when in fact he is winning by exploiting a weakness of yours that allows him to use his strength.

The lesson is that to move up a level, you need to improve your overall game, not just one aspect. A player who is a level stronger than you rarely defeats you with one aspect of his game (although many erroneously believe this to be true); he does so by improving the overall level of his game. (There are, of course, players who have improved all but one aspect of their game, and by improving that one final aspect, suddenly go up the coveted level!) A strength in your game can compensate for a weakness, but only to a certain extent.

So how do you go about improving the overall level of your game? To move up a level in table tennis, you have to be able to match the players a level higher than you on five key things:

1. You have to return your opponents' serves as well as they return your serves.
2. You have to either rally as fast as your opponents can rally, or force your opponents to rally at your pace (by slowing the pace down with pushes, slow loops, controlled drives, etc.). ("Pace" means both speed and quickness.)
3. You have to be able to react to your opponents' rallying spins (loops, pushes, chops, lobs, spins returned by long pips, etc.) as well as they react to yours.
4. You have to be able to end the point (i.e. smashing, loop kills) as well as your opponents do. (This means either being able to end the point as well as your opponents, or being able to stop them from ending the point better than you can by not giving them shots where they can end the point. Ending the point does not always mean ending it with one shot – it can also mean a series of strong shots that win the point.)
5. And finally, you have to have at least one strength that threatens your opponents as much as their strengths threaten you, and a way of getting your strength(s) into play.

You may have noted that tactics is not one of the five "keys." This is because tactics is part of all five keys. Stronger/weaker tactics simply make you stronger/weaker in each key.

Do some (but not all) of the above five keys, and your performance in a tournament will go up some, perhaps half a level, but not a full level. Developing a single "overpowering" strength won't raise your level as much as you'd think, as opponents a level higher will beat you on the less developed parts of your game. Even players at your "previous" level will still often beat you by exploiting these weaknesses. But ... if you improve all five things, even just a little bit, you'll improve dramatically.

What's stronger, a chain with four powerful links and one weak one, or a chain with five pretty strong ones?

July 14, 2014 – The 7 Habits of Highly Effective Table Tennis Players

There's a best-selling book called *The 7 Habits of Highly Effective People*. The book lists these as the "7 Habits": 1) Be proactive; 2) Begin with the End in Mind; 3) Put First Things First; 4) Think Win/Win; 5) Seek First to Understand, Then to Be Understood; 6) Synergize; and 7) Sharpen the Saw. (There's also a best-selling sort of sequel from the same author, "The 7 Habits of Highly Effective Teens.")

These books have had a major impact on many people's lives. And there's a correlation between some of these and the habits of "highly effective table tennis players." For example, you don't get to be a top player without being proactive, i.e. striving to do what it takes to improve. However, I'm not going to try to create a one-to-one correlation between the seven habits listed and ones used by top table tennis players. Instead, I'm going to provide my own list of seven habits of "highly effective table tennis players." Follow these 7 habits, and see how it improves your game. On the following page is my list.

Let's all practice together!

123

The 7 Habits of Highly Effective Table Tennis Players

1. **Loves to practice.**

   It's not enough to just put in the motions. You have to *want* to improve, and want to so badly that you love practicing as it allows you to do what you want to do. Going through the motions with your mind blankly just going along is a waste of time. If you love to practice, you'll improve far faster than one who is just doing the motions.

2. **Proactive in finding ways to improve, strategically and tactically.**

   Strategic thinking is about developing your game for the future. Tactical thinking is about developing the habit of winning with what you have. You need to learn both, and you need to take the initiative in doing so. Don't leave this to your opponents, who will happily figure it out for you while beating you in competition. But when they do beat you, that's the feedback you need to analyze so you can find ways to improve.

3. **Is working toward specific goals, both short-, intermediate-, and long-term.**

   Mindless practice is just that – mindless. Decide what you need to work on, and focus on that like a laser.

4. **A perfectionist in most or all aspects of the game.**

   If you strive for perfection, you'll come a lot closer than one who strives for something less.

5. **Never gives up, whether in tournaments or practice.**

   Fighters do a lot better than those who don't have a burning desire to win every point.

6. **Loves to compete and win.**

   If winning isn't fun, then why are you practicing? Sure, you could be practicing just for the sake of having better shots or for exercise, but this isn't about the "seven habits of highly effective exercisers or having better shots without trying to become a better player."

7. **Respects opponent's game while looking to dominate it.**

   If you don't respect an opponent's game, it's hard to try your best against it.

June 16, 2014 – Be a Perfectionist

If you want to be very good at table tennis or anything else, it's best to be a perfectionist. But to be a perfectionist, you have to think like a perfectionist.

First, focus on getting it right. In the long run, proper execution is more important than any current result, and proper execution will lead to the best results. So focus on the techniques that are "perfect," and work to replicate them over and over until you can do them in your sleep, as well as at deuce in the fifth.

Second, forget about the incorrect shots as those are the shots you want out of your head. Thinking about them only ingrains them more. Instead, develop a determination to do the *next* shot "perfectly." If you keep doing the shot incorrectly, then you might have to analyze it to figure out what you need to do, but as soon as you get it right, put the incorrect ones out of your head and focus on doing it correctly.

Third, don't try to memorize the specifics of a "perfect" shot. Instead, once you get it right, remember the feel of the shot. Once you have that feel down, it'll feel wrong anytime you do any part of the stroke incorrectly. Getting the feel right will ingrain the shot not just for now, but for a lifetime.

If you really want to get it right, I strongly urge you to find a coach and have him work with you until you get it right, and have the feel of a "perfect" shot. Once you have that, you can practice the shot on your own without worrying about whether you are doing it right.

April 21, 2014 – Every Battle Is Won Before the Battle Begins

The title is a famous quote from Sun Tzu, the famous Chinese military strategist and philosopher. It's from his book "The Art of War," but much of it equally applies to sports. This quote capsulizes what should be obvious to table tennis players – that a match is, indeed, won before it begins. Let's look at what goes into winning a match.

First off is your **equipment**. That is chosen before the match begins.

Next are your **techniques**, the most important aspect. This means your strokes, serves, receive, and footwork. But these are all developed before the match begins.

Next is the **physical aspect**. Again, any physical training is done in advance, and other aspects (height, age, health and injuries, etc.) are also determined before the match begins.

Then there's the **mental aspect**, perhaps the most varied part from match to match. But any mental training (or lack thereof) also comes before the match. Even if you haven't had any mental training, the mental habits you pick up are pretty much set before the match begins. If you are the nervous type who falls apart under pressure, then you were the nervous wreck who falls apart under pressure before the match began. If you are the type who is cool under pressure and plays great when the match is on the line, you were that way coming into the match. If you want to change or improve these aspects, you need to do it before the match.

Finally, there is your **tactical game**. But again, your tactical skills (or lack thereof) were developed before the match. If you have a coach, that is normally arranged before the match. And if you want to scout your opponent out before the match starts or talk to someone who knows the player, and develop a tactical plan, that too takes place before the match.

Now anyone can get technical and point out that no matter how much preparation you do there is still some randomness – nets and edges, how well the opponent plays, even the accuracy of advice given from others. But while these are unknowns going into the match, it is your preparation before the match that sets the chances of your winning, given the circumstances. This includes the mental aspect (see above), the part that most varies from match to match for most players. Players are often stronger mentally in some matches than others – which really shows a mental weakness in the times when they are not mentally strong, something that can be overcome with sports psychology training. But the preparation before the match sets the odds of being mentally strong in a given match. Perhaps the article could better be titled, "The Odds of Winning a Match Are Set Before the Match Begins." But in the long run, it's the same thing.

So the next time you are getting ready to play a tournament, don't worry about how well you'll play. Worry about how well you've prepared.

June 6, 2016 – What to Focus on to Improve

At different levels, players need to focus on different things to improve. Here's a rundown.

- **Beginners**: Fundamentals, Fundamentals, Fundamentals! I can't get any more specific than that. Develop those fundamentals until you can do them in your sleep —strokes, footwork, serve, and receive. Work with a coach to develop them, find players to practice with, and drill, drill, drill!

- **Advanced Beginner**: Playing Style. At this point you have at least semi-mastered the basic fundamentals, and should be looking to develop a winning playing style. But keep harping on those Fundamentals, Fundamentals, Fundamentals!

- **Intermediate**: You now have a playing style and have somewhat mastered the fundamentals. Now you should be really honing your playing style, as in what shots you should do and when. Your serve and receive game should directly be setting up your game. You should be figuring out what you win and lose on, and work to get rid of weaknesses while making your strengths overpowering. But guess what? You still are not advanced, and so you need to continue to focus on those Fundamentals, Fundamentals, Fundamentals!

- **Advanced**: You have mastered the fundamentals, though (brace yourself) you should continue to work on them as long as you want to improve – the more consistent they are, the better you will be. But you also need to really develop all parts of your game so that you are the master of any situation and against any style. You need to constantly examine your game and your matches and figure out what you are winning and losing on, and train to overcome any weaknesses while continuing to develop overpowering strengths. You have fewer rivals now – you've left most past ones behind – so at this point you should be studying your rivals to find specific ways to defeat them.

August 3, 2015 – Get to the Root of the Problem

Many coaches and players try to fix problems by fixing the symptoms. In many ways, this is what separates a good, experienced coach from, say, a top player who knows proper technique but isn't that experienced in coaching it.

Here's an example. Suppose a player tends to fall back as they loop forehands. The "simple" solution, of course, is to tell them to focus on rotating around and forward into the ball, i.e. "don't fall back." And many coaches try this many times, and it doesn't work – because they are treating a *symptom* of a problem rather than the *root* of the problem. The real question is *why* is the player falling backwards? – and the answer almost every time is that he's too far from the ball, with his left leg too far from the table. And so he's forced to reach a bit forward. The falling back is to keep his balance. Solution: Have the player stand closer to the ball, with the left leg closer to the table. Then he'll have a natural rotation into and through the ball, with no falling backwards and off balance afterwards.

Here's another. Some players struggle to rotate their body backwards (to the right for righties) on the forehand. The more they try, the more awkward they look. I've seen coaches struggle with this, not being able to figure out why the player has so much trouble with something that's so easy for others. And so they'll keep telling the player to rotate more on the forehand. But the player simply can't do the rotation comfortably – the *symptom* of a problem – because they haven't fixed the *root* of the problem – which usually is their knees are facing forward. If you watch top players, the knees point somewhat outward in their ready stance, which allows easy rotation in either direction. Here's an example – see how the knees point somewhat sideways, not forward? www.experttabletennis.com/wp-content/uploads/2013/03/table-tennis-stance.jpg

And here's another. Often players struggle to get great spin on their serves. Rather than converting most of their energy into spin, and getting slow but super-spinny serves, their serves go long, with only moderate spin. Often they are told to graze the ball more, but when they try, they are unable to do so – because the inability to graze the ball is a *symptom* of a problem, not the *root* of the problem. The root of the problem usually is they are contacting the back of the ball, often toward the top. If they want to graze the ball more, they need to contact more under the ball and more on the side. If the player doesn't change his contact point, he'll continue to struggle to graze the ball as his racket will be approaching the ball too directly to graze the ball, resulting in a flatter contact. You can still get moderate spin this way, and many players (and coaches) settle for that, never realizing how they are limiting themselves.

October 5, 2015 – Serving and the Snowball Effect

One of the best ways to dramatically improve your game is to develop serves that lead to developing other aspects of your game. The stronger serves and developing other aspects of your game lead to a higher level of play, meaning you get to play stronger opponents, which leads to further improvement. The stronger opponents force you to continue to develop the serves and other aspects of your game, leading to a snowballing effect that can, over time, dramatically improve your level of play.

I'm going to use my experience with this as an example. During my first few years I focused a lot on developing my serves. The result was I would get lots of relatively weak returns to attack. This developed both my attack and my footwork, which made me better both on my serve as well as in rallies. Because I became dominant on my serve and my attacks and footwork improved because of my serve, my overall level improved, and I began playing stronger players. Going up against better players pushed me to even higher levels. I was forced to improve my serve even more to keep them effective against stronger players. Since I had developed a strong serve and attack, as I played better players who received my serves better, I was forced to continue to improve my attack and footwork. The result? By developing my serves early on it snowballed my development. I was able to go from beginner to 1900 in about two and a half years, and 2100 in five. (With rating inflation, that's more like 2000 and 2200.)

So what does this mean for you? Develop strong serves that allow you to consistently serve and attack. Such serves don't have to give you easy pop-ups; it's sufficient that they consistently give you balls you can attack, while forcing a number of "free" points as opponents make mistakes (often from trying to receive so you can't attack). Develop both third-ball attack serves (that allow you to consistently serve and attack) and a few "trick" serves (that give you free points if not overused – most such serves become ineffective after a few usages). Learn to serve with great spin and deception (including no-spin serves that look spinny), both short and long, to all parts of the table, with different serving motions. If you aren't sure how to do these serves, talk to a coach or top player.

March 31, 2014 – Get the Right Feel

The worst thing a coach can do is try to fill a player's head with all sorts of things he must do to get a shot right, and the worst thing a player can do is try to memorize all these things. A coach might look at a player and see several things that need fixing. But the last thing he wants is for the student to have to be thinking something like, "Let's see, my feet need to be like this, my arm like this, I have to rotate this way, keeping the racket at this height and my elbow bent this much, and then I need to start the swing with this part of my body, followed by that part, then that part, and finally that part, and make sure contact is like this, and then follow through so my racket goes here." That's how you might program a computer, but not a human brain!!!

Instead, the goal of a player (and therefore the goal of the coach) is to find the right "feel" of the shot. If all the aspects of a short are done properly, it should feel right, and once a player does a shot just right (perhaps with a coach pointing out the "right" ones), the player should never memorize all the aspects that went into making the shot right. He just needs to remember the feel of the shot – the feel of the stroke, the contact, and the timing, all of which go together.

Once a player gets the feel right, all he has to do is repeat that feel over and over, with minor changes based on the incoming shot that mostly affect racket angle. At its most basic level, that's all there is to learning a new technique – getting the feel right, and then repeating it. However, it's not always that easy. Two common problems are 1) getting the feel right when there are two or more things wrong, and 2) getting the right feel for forehand and backhand shots while using mostly the same grip.

Often a player has trouble doing proper technique because he's doing two or more things wrong, leading to an awkward but at least workable shot. If the player tries to fix one of the problems, the stroke falls apart unless he simultaneously fixes the other problem(s), which can be difficult to do together. For example, a player may have an improper grip, leading to an awkward stroking technique. But if he fixes the grip, it messes up the timing in the awkward stroking technique, and so the player gets worse, not better. The player has to both change the grip and the stroking technique at the same time. To do this takes practice, often with a coach – but once done properly, the player can remember the "feel" of the proper grip and stroke, and then he can learn to do it over and over.

Often a player learns the right feel for a forehand and backhand shot, but with different grips. This doesn't always work – it takes time to grip change, and so most players use mostly the same grip for forehand and backhand shots, with only minor changes. So a player needs to not only get the right feel for each shot, but the right feel using a grip that can be used for other shots, with perhaps some minor grip changes. (Some players, such as former world #1 Timo Boll, uses bigger grip changes, so this is something others might want to develop.)

So focus on getting the right feel for your shots, and it'll feel more and more natural as you develop the timing – and soon you'll be feeling (and playing) like a champion!

June 29, 2015 – The Feel of a Shot and a Checklist

When learning new techniques, many players make the mistake of trying to remember the specifics of each shot. While this is important to know later as a checklist to go over when the shot is off, this is not the way to learn a new technique. Instead, your goal is to get the shot right *one time*, and then remember the feel of that shot – the stroke and contact – and then repeat. If you get the feel right, all the specifics will fall into place.

When your shots aren't working and it doesn't feel right, that's when you might need to go through a short checklist for the new technique to find out what's wrong. But again, the goal is to get the feel right, and then put the checklist aside.

So learn both the feel and the specifics of each new technique you learn, and write the latter down – that's an assignment – and then forget about them and focus on the feel. When the feel is right, so will the technique. When the feel is wrong, and you can't figure out why, that's when you pull out your checklist to get back to the right feel.

July 13, 2015 – Change and the Definition of Insanity

Insanity is often defined as doing the same thing over and over again and expecting a different result. In some contexts, this might not seem to make sense. If you are learning something new in table tennis and can't get it right, you keep doing it over and over until you do get it right. However, the key point is this – if you are learning something new and keep missing, that means you are doing something *wrong*, and until you change that, you'll keep missing.

Change is the key when learning. And yet, over and over, players do the same old things and expect different results. I'll watch players lose because they keep blocking an opponent's loop off the end, and then, instead of doing some saturation training (where you focus on one thing for a time to get it right) to fix their blocking, they'll go practice what they've always practiced – looping, hitting, whatever – and of course that's why they are strong on the things they practice a lot, and not strong on the things they don't practice as much. Or they'll be unable to return a certain serve, and yet, when it's over, rather than find someone who can do that serve so they can practice against it, they'll practice the same things they've always practiced. They won't even try to learn the serve that gave them trouble, when of course it might be a weapon they could use against others.

So go take a good, hard look at your game. What problems do you see? What can you change to fix them? Perhaps ask a coach or knowledgeable player the same question. Then address the problem.

August 8, 2016 – Three Weapons: The Triple B's

You have three weapons in table tennis – your Body, your Brain, and your Bat. The last is the least important. You can go to any club and try out others rackets and find the right fit, and you're done in one night. (Sorry, Equipment Junkies.) But the others take years to develop.

Your body is the second most important. At the higher levels, this becomes increasingly important. You can't throw yourself into shot after shot like an Olympian without having at least some minimal physical fitness. And yet there are players who play at a very high level who would never be mistaken for Olympians. And how do they do this? They use their most important asset.

Your brain is your most important asset in table tennis. It controls everything you do, either consciously or subconsciously. Consciously it decides how often you practice, what you practice, and how hard you practice. It makes the strategic long-term decisions on how to develop your game, and the short-term tactical decisions that make the most of what you have. Subconsciously it controls (or should control) all your shots from the serve to the actual strokes and racket angles. (That's why you train, so you can do these things automatically, i.e. subconsciously.) Table tennis is rightfully called "chess at light speed." It is the brainiest of sports.

Are you making full use of your brain?

May 2, 2016 – React to Opponent's Swing

When a player hits the ball very hard at a top player, often the top player effortlessly returns these shots as if he has reflexes far beyond those of normal people. This isn't really true. In fact, in non-table tennis things, where he hasn't trained for many years, he might have only average reflexes. And yet he seems to react instantly to these smashes and loop kills. How does he do this?

From years of training, a top player develops fast reactions to things they train for. You could argue they have faster reflexes in table tennis and be correct, but only for those things they have trained for.

But there's a second thing going on here. Most players barely react to an opponent's shot until the ball is coming toward them, or at most at the last second as the opponent hits the ball. But the reality is that the huge majority of the time you can judge where the ball is going and how fast almost the instant the opponent starts his forward swing. If you watch top players react to smashes and loop kills, watch how they begin to move into position as the opponent begins that forward swing – it's almost as if they know where the ball is going to be hit – because they do. (Not consciously, of course; it's all trained subconscious, i.e. muscle memory.)

How can you do this? It's all about observing the opponent, and learning to react to his movements. Just as you learn to subconsciously react to an opponent's spin based on his movements, you should learn to make the connection between an opponent's swing and the direction the ball will go, as well as its speed, spin, trajectory, etc., so that reacting to it becomes second-nature. You may have to observe this consciously at first, but soon it becomes a subconscious habit.

For example, you can read much about the direction an opponent is about to go by watching his shoulders. So be aware of the opponent's shoulders, and you will develop the proper reactions to his shots, reacting faster and faster. It's not about having faster reflexes; it's about developing proper reactions that just make you *appear* to have fast reflexes.

March 28, 2016 – Stroke Technique vs. Consistency, Serve, and Receive

Many players constantly obsess over their strokes, rightfully wanting to have "perfect technique." While that's admirable, it often keeps them from reaching their full potential. Why? Because the obsession with perfect technique often comes at the expense of developing consistency, serves, and receive. (Plus, what is "perfect technique"? Not all of the best players have the same technique.

Especially for players who have played a long time, trying to change technique is difficult and time-consuming. Instead, assuming the players had pretty good technique, the time might instead be used for developing consistency with those techniques, developing great serves, and mastering receive. If players obsessed over these as much as having "perfect technique," many would reach higher levels.

This doesn't mean one shouldn't try to develop great technique – but it's all about the law of diminishing returns. Kids, and beginners without bad habits already ingrained, should focus on great technique. Others might settle for good (or perhaps very good) technique – and then, by using that technique for years, develop consistency without going for that elusive "perfect technique." Meanwhile, few players really develop their serves to a high level, and even fewer become good at receive, which is often called "everyone's weakness."

So if you have good technique, discuss with a coach the relative advantages of going for perfect technique in limited practice time, versus working toward consistency, serve, and receive. Because guess what? Most matches below the highest levels are won on those three.

May 25, 2015 – Performance vs. Results

Far too many players judge themselves by their results rather than their performance. While it's importance to use results as goals, all you can really control is your performance. What's the difference?

Performance is what you do. Results are what happens based on the performances of both you and your opponent, as well as perhaps some luck. (Bad luck comes in many ways, such as nets and edges; bad draws, such as drawing a playing style you don't play well against; or ill-timed injuries or illnesses.)

It's normal to be unhappy with a poor result. But there's a huge difference between a high-performance loss and low-performance win. You need to judge them separately. There really are four possibilities:

1. Happy with result/happy with performance
2. Happy with result/unhappy with performance
3. Unhappy with result/happy with performance
4. Unhappy with result/unhappy with performance

The **first case** is win-win – go celebrate! Have a hot fudge banana split. That doesn't mean you can relax and rest on your laurels. You might be able to coast and keep your current performance level, but guess what? The players you beat are all gunning for you, and will likely raise their performance, especially against you. So if you want to keep the same result, you need to continue to improve your performance.

The **second case** is cause for celebration, but should leave you determined to play better. No hot fudge on your ice cream. You won, and should be happy with this result, but know you should have performed better. Perhaps you won because the other guy didn't perform well enough or perhaps you got lucky. You should celebrate the win, but be dying to get to the playing hall to practice and get your performance to where it should be.

The **third case** is bittersweet. You played well, and yet you lost. Have some plain vanilla ice cream. Now you have to make a calculation: Do you want to put in the effort needed to improve your performance to the point where you *might* change the result? There are no guarantees; you may practice and train with the best coaches and still lose, even to the same player who might also improve his performance. But guess what? If you put in the time, your chances of changing the result to a win go up dramatically. And even if you don't change the result in question, you'll be a better player, and you will have better results overall.

The **fourth case** is the toughest. You played poorly and of course have nothing to celebrate. No ice cream for you. You know you could have played better. You should be dying to get to the playing hall so you can practice and eventually put in the performance you know you can do. You may or may not change the result, but you'll at least be satisfied that you did your best – and your chances of the changing the result to a win go up dramatically.

In all four cases, you need to examine the match, see where you won and lost, and practice to improve your performance in both of those areas for next time. Bottom line: Judge your performance by your actual performance, and use results as goals to reach by improving your performance.

March 30, 2015 – Technical Problems Often Come in Pairs

If you think about it, this is somewhat obvious – and yet most don't really think about it when fixing a technique, leading to great difficulties in making these changes. They'll try to fix one part of the technique, but unless they fix both parts at the same time, the technique won't work properly.

Imagine a player with perfect technique. Now imagine changing something so his technique is no longer perfect. He'll likely have to compensate somewhere else in his technique for this change or his shots will no longer hit the table. Similarly, a player with one poor part of his technique will almost always have at least one other poor part to compensate.

For example, let's suppose a player's backswing is too short on a loop. To compensate, the player will likely swing more violently to gain the racket speed, leading to a poorly-controlled jerky stroke. To fix this he has to both extend the backswing while slowing down the acceleration to a smoothly controlled swing.

Or suppose a player hits or loops forehands with his right foot (for righties) too far back. To compensate he'll likely have less waist rotation (since otherwise he'll literally be facing backwards during the backswing), leading to an awkward and less-powerful stroke. To fix the problem he has to both bring the right foot a bit more forward while increasing the waist rotation.

Or suppose the opposite, that the player hits or loops forehand with his right foot slightly forward (i.e. a backhand position) or even with the left foot (for a player who doesn't have a supple waist and/or spend many hours each week training like top players who correctly do this). The player will likely find it difficult to rotate the body properly in the time needed in a rally, and so will tend to stroke with only the upper body and arm, again leading to an awkward and less-powerful stroke. To fix the problem he has to both adjust the foot position and increase the body rotation. (Note how both improper foot positions lead to difficulties with using the lower body and proper body rotation.)

The same is true of a player who plays with his two feet parallel to each other, which makes it harder to rotate the lower body, and so leads again to an awkward and less-powerful stroke. Again, both the foot position and the body rotation need to be adjusted. Telling him to do one without the other won't help.

Or imagine a player who stands too far off the table when forehand looping against backspin, a common problem. He'll have to reach forward too much in his swing, and so to keep his balance will have to pull back with his left side, and so fall backwards slightly, leading to a loss of power and balance. Telling the player not to fall backward won't help unless you also tell him to stand closer to the table. His contact point with the ball may be the same, but it won't be so far in front of him.

Another common problem is the player who lifts his elbow during his forehand drive, leading to the racket angle changing from too open to closed during the stroke, making it hard to control what the angle is right at contact. If you tell him to stop lifting the elbow without also focusing on starting the forward swing with the racket at the proper angle he'll have great difficulties.

Sometimes there are more than two roots to the problem. If a player stands up too straight, this forces all sorts of adjustments to compensate. When the player tries to stay lower with a wider stance and knees more bent (as he should), he'll have to change a number of aspects (for the better) to his stroking technique. But if he doesn't make these changes, his new stance and stroking techniques will be awkward.

There are many more examples like this. What technique problems do you have in your game, and is the root of the problem singular or plural?

February 2, 2015 – Develop the Five Types of Rallying Shots

There really are only five types of rallying shots, and you should perfect them all. If you can't, your game is not complete and you'll never be as good as you could be. So what are these five types of shots you should develop?

1. **Opening Attacks**

   These are your first attacks in a rally. Against a ball that goes long this usually means looping, though you can also do a more simple drive. Against a short ball this means a flip (usually called a flick in Europe). A surprising number of seemingly defensive or passive players actually have good attacks once they are into the rally, but they don't have effective or consistent opening attacks, and so they are usually on the defensive.

2. **Continuing Attacks**

   It's not enough to open with an attack; you have to continue the attack. At the higher levels this usually means to loop over and over. You can also continue your attack with regular drives, which is especially common on the backhand. This is often the most physically demanding aspect of table tennis as you are forced to move quickly to keep up an attack.

3. **Putaways**

   If you can't end the point when the shot is there, then you are severely handicapped. This means loop kills and smashes. (One of the best ways to develop your putaway shots is with multiball practice.)

4. **Consistency**

   The game isn't all attack. Consistency shots include regular drives, blocks, steady loops, pushing, as well as defensive off-table shots chopping, lobbing, and fishing. There is overlap here with "Continuing Attacks" as a steady loop can fit both categories. Consistency shots are best used at the start of the rally to return serves (such as pushing or a soft-to-medium-speed loop) and to withstand an opponent's attack.

5. **Tricky Shots**

   These are the often unorthodox shots, ones where you throw something different at an opponent to make him uncomfortable. Examples would be a change of pace, drop shot, no-spin shots that look like spin, an unexpectedly heavy spin (such as a very heavy push), an unexpected sidespin (such as a sidespin block or loop, both of which you can sidespin either way), or a last-second change of direction. You probably don't want to center your game around these types of shots, but if you don't have at least a small arsenal of tricky shots to throw off an opponent then you are handicapping yourself. Even all-out attackers use such tricky shots on occasion, such as on receive, with sidespin loops, or sudden changes of direction.

Now examine your game, and ask yourself which of the above are you very good at? You can develop your game around these shots. However, the more important question is probably which of them are you weak at? (Rather than rate them relative to your current level, rate them relative to the level you are striving to reach.) Now you know what to work on. Go to it.

January 5, 2015 – Hitting or Looping?

In the past this was always a difficult question – should you be a hitter or a looper? It's a difficult question for many at the non-elite levels, but at higher levels there's not much question anymore – pretty much everyone is a looper. (When I refer to hitting, that includes blocking, so perhaps it would be better called a "hitter/blocker." Of course loopers also block, but not as much as a hitter/blocker style player.)

Unless your goal is to be a world-class player (say, top 100 in the world), you can go either way. Players who start out young, once they've developed the basics, should probably focus on looping as their potential is high. Players who start older can also loop, but let's face it – if you start, say, in your thirties or forties, you are unlikely to be world-class. In this case it's a question of where are you more talented, and what do you prefer?

If you want to play the way the world-class players play – style-wise, not necessarily level-wise – then become a looper. If you have loose, relaxed muscles, looping will also be easier. Bigger, stronger players also tend to find looping easier. On the other hand, if you are very quick, then perhaps hitting is your forte. In some ways it's a dying style as few coaches teach it anymore except to older players – but that's also an advantage as players aren't used to playing this type of style as much as in the past. You might even consider using short pips, and really mess up some players who only know how to play inverted.

Whichever you go for, turn your looping or hitting into a weapon. Develop your serve, receive, and rallying shots to set up this shot. You want it to be a terror for opponents, who lose points both to that shot and in their attempts to not set the shot up for you – a double whammy. Perhaps work with a coach or top player on the shot, use it every chance you can in drills and games, and whether you are looping or hitting soon you'll have a true weapon.

April 28, 2014 – Develop the Fundamentals: Strokes & Footwork

At the 2004 USA Nationals, Cheng Yinghua, 46, became the oldest Men's Singles Champion in history, and the four semifinalists averaged over 40 years old. This was unique in a sport that is usually dominated by younger, faster players. When asked what the younger players needed to do to compete with these veterans, four-time U.S. Men's champ and full-time coach Cheng said, "The younger players had not put enough training time and effort into the fundamentals.

Fundamentals, fundamentals, fundamentals.

Some find them boring, but they are probably the three most important things in being a Champion. No one becomes a champion in this sport without a solid foundation in the fundamentals.

Many find it the "boring" part of training, since fundamentals are mostly developed through repetition, but they are absolutely necessary.

Fundamentals, fundamentals, fundamentals.

They don't need to be boring. At the beginning level, where repetition isn't easy, it should be a challenge just to do the repeating strokes. As players advance, they should work in more and more advanced drills, which leads both to more advanced play and more interesting practice.

- **What are the Fundamentals?**

The fundamentals include both proper stroking and footwork technique. Tactics, mental and physical conditioning, even great serve and receive don't help a lot if you don't have the fundamentals down.

At its most basic level, table tennis involves moving into position, and then stroking the ball. Along the way, you have to choose which stroke to use, read the incoming ball and adjust the stroke and racket angle to it. But if you can't move and stroke properly, nothing will help you.

The actual specifics of how to move and stroke are outside the scope of this article. For these, you really need a coach, although videos and books can also help. (Yes, it would take an entire book to cover the fundamentals.) You can find coaches at www.usatt.org/coaching. You can find books and videos from most major table tennis dealers.

The purpose of fundamentals is to develop consistency in your shots. To be consistent, you need to both be in position for each shot, and use the same repeating strokes over and over. That's what fundamentals are all about.

- **Footwork Fundamentals**

To be a Champion, you have to develop proper footwork so that you are able to catch every ball in your forehand or backhand hitting zones.

Some players just stand at the table, and reach for the ball. If the ball just happens to be in the perhaps one-foot area that's convenient for their strokes, they hit a good shot. If it's outside that area, they have to adjust their shot – and so lose consistency. A good opponent will rarely hit a ball that you don't have to move to.

- **Stroking Fundamentals**

    To be a Champion, you have to develop repeating strokes, strokes that you can do over and over and over and (my God!) over and over and over. At the advanced level, this means many strokes, including forehand and backhand drives, loops, blocks, pushes, flips, and perhaps even lobbing and chopping. It's hard enough learning all these shots against all the different incoming balls (different spins, speeds, depth, direction, height, etc.). Now imagine having to do so while changing your stroke each time! Instead, develop a simple repeating stroke, and then all you have to do is essentially adjust the racket angle and perhaps the trajectory of the stroke.

- **Beginning Fundamentals**

    Many coaches swear by the "100" theory – you don't work on much of anything else until you can do 100 forehand and 100 backhand drives with a proper stroke. To a beginner, this is a real challenge, and should be an exciting challenge. The same is true of each of the other strokes – they are a challenge at the beginning level, and striving to do a certain number in a row is a challenge. As the stroke is learned, the fundamental footwork should be learned with footwork drills, so moving to each ball and stroking it properly becomes … fundamental.

    For each new drill involving a new stroke or some combination of stroking and footwork, beginners can see how many they can do in a row. It's an exciting challenge, and sometimes they forget along the way that they are getting better and better!

- **Intermediate & Advanced Fundamentals**

At the intermediate level, the player can do all the strokes consistently with proper repeating strokes. At this point, it's time to get the fundamentals into game-like situations. This means doing drills that include more and more variation, and more and more random drills. Random drills are where the player doesn't always know where the ball is going. If the fundamentals are mastered, a player can do this, at least at a slower pace. As the player advances, the speed of the drill can speed up. All players have a maximum speed at which they can still maintain the fundamentals; if you go beyond that speed, their fundamentals break down. By drilling, drilling, and more drilling, a player can increase the speed at which they can execute the fundamentals.

- **Putting it Together**

Table tennis has been called chess at hyper speed. Imagine playing chess where you were missing a rook or queen. That's what playing with poor fundamentals is. Proper fundamentals mean knowing you can execute the shots you call for in any given situation.

Fundamentals, fundamentals, fundamentals.

The Chinese tend to dominate table tennis worldwide. Most coaches would say that ultimately, the biggest advantage they have over their opponents is stronger fundamentals. It may be fun to play games, and they are important to improving, but the best players spend the majority of their training on … you guessed it, fundamentals. They may do it at a pace that doesn't seem very fundamental, but that's because of years and years of developing these fundamentals until they can do them at that pace. Why are they still working on them? So they can do them consistently at an even faster pace against anything an opponent can throw at them.

If you want to be a Champion, you'll do the same.

March 24, 2014 – Isolating Techniques and Combinations

One of the more important concepts you should use in your training is to isolate specific techniques so you can work on them. At its most simple you work on individual shots, such as a forehand or backhand drive, loop, or push. Most players understand this and spend countless hours perfecting these shots.

However, once these shots are perfected in practice, should you go straight to matches? Probably not. Instead, the next step would be to isolate various combinations. For example, many players regularly loop against backspin, and then follow with a loop or smash against the likely blocked return. First you'd want to develop the loop against backspin, and the loop or smash against block. But once you have these two shots down, it's time to put them together. For example, you do a drill where you serve backspin to your partner's backhand; he pushes it back to a pre-set spot (such as your middle backhand); you loop a forehand (or backhand) to your partner's backhand; he blocks to your forehand; then you loop or smash that ball anywhere, and then it's free play until the rally ends. As simple as this is, this is one of the most important drills for most developing players.

Another example might be to have your partner push and then block to your backhand, and you backhand loop the first (or drive, if that's how you attack backspin), and follow with a backhand loop or drive against the block, then free play. This backhand one-two combo is extremely valuable and comes up in matches all the time, and yet many players fail to practice it.

There are many other examples, though opening against a backspin and following up against a block is probably the most common. The key here is that you have to lift some against the backspin, while you don't lift much against the follow-up shot against a block, but unless you practice it, you might find yourself accidentally lifting the second ball and watching it go off the end.

If you are a hitter you might serve fast topspin to your partner's backhand; your partner counter-hits back your backhand; you backhand hit to your partner's backhand (or some other pre-set spot), he counter-hits to your backhand again (not too hard), and you step around and smash a forehand, then it's free play.

You can also add some serve and receive. For example, have your partner serve short backspin to your forehand (or backhand); you push back to a preset spot (and perhaps push short); your partner pushes to your backhand; you backhand loop. Or some other version of this.

You can also add some more randomness to the drills. For example, you serve backspin to your partner's backhand, he pushes back randomly anywhere on the table, you loop (forehand or backhand) to his

144

backhand, and he blocks either randomly or to a pre-set spot, and then free play. Or, if you do that drill well, go random on this drill from the start. If you are a hitter serving fast topspin, your partner can return anywhere and you have to follow with a smash, forehand or backhand. (Note – there aren't too many pure hitters at the higher levels anymore, alas.)

Think about your game and what types of shots and combinations you use (or should be using). Isolate two shots that you commonly do in combination. Then design a drill for those two shots and go out and practice!

March 3, 2014 – Changing Bad Technique

How does one go about changing bad technique? Most players use halfway measures, and when that doesn't work, they give up and go back to their old habits. They may try minor adjustments when a major one is needed. They may change from one poor technique to another. They may practice it properly, but then, before the proper technique is ingrained, they'll play competitive matches and fall back into old habits, thereby re-ingraining the poor technique. They may have an improper grip or stance which causes the poor technique. Or they simply don't know what needs to be fixed. How can you overcome this? Here are five recommendations.

First, drop out of tournaments and match play for a while and focus on fixing the technique. Hit regularly with a coach or practice partner as you fix the technique. Playing matches will just reinforce the bad technique. If your goal is to really overcome poor technique and replace it with good technique, then you need to have an extended period where you focus on this, i.e. saturation training. That means only playing with a coach or practice partner, and doing drills where you can isolate the new technique so you can focus on doing it correctly.

Second, exaggerate the proper technique. If you don't rotate your shoulders enough on a shot, practice over-rotating until it becomes comfortable to do it the proper way. Shadow practice the proper technique over and Over and OVER until you can do it in your sleep, on your deathbed, and most importantly, at deuce in the fifth.

Third, watch top players (live or on video) who do the stroke well, and visualize yourself doing it that way. The more you visualize it done properly, the more likely you'll do it properly. Then shadow stroke it as you visualize it.

Fourth, make sure your grip and stance are correct. If you get these two correct, then everything in between tends to fall into place. If you get one of them wrong, then fixing a problem somewhere else won't work unless you fix the root cause of the problem – the grip or stance.

Fifth, work with a coach. Fixing bad technique is his job. Let him do his job.

Let me emphasize item #1 above. In general it's best to play lots of matches and get as much tournament competition as possible when trying to improve (along with lots of regular practice, i.e. drills), but when you are making major changes to your game, it's best to take time off from competition. Perhaps set a goal to have your game ready for tournament competition for a specific tournament (or series of tournaments) six months or so away, and train specifically for that. I don't think you need to take six months off from playing practice matches, but perhaps two months of focused practice without matches would greatly help you in making these technique changes.

January 25, 2016 – Should You Develop Your Forehand Push?

At the lower levels, pushing is often over-used, but at the higher levels, many underestimate their value. All top players have excellent pushes. However, advanced players – and even intermediate players – rarely push against deep backspin to the forehand, unless they are choppers. (And even choppers will often attack them.) It's simply better for them to attack, usually with a loop. (The same can be said on the backhand, if you have a good backhand loop.) So ... should you develop your forehand push?

The answer is yes – but not necessarily against long backspin to the forehand. You need to develop your forehand push mostly against short backspin to the forehand. Against this ball, you can attack, but pushing is often the better bet. You can push short, push quick and long, go for angles, heavy spin, etc. – all sorts of variations. And because you are closer to your opponent, he has less time to react. (At the same time, don't predictably push – learn to flip short balls as well.)

The problem is how do you practice your forehand push? If you push forehand to forehand with a partner, then unless both of you are practicing short pushes, you'll be practicing pushing against long balls. The answer is to develop the forehand push this way with a partner, but once it becomes relatively advanced, start focusing on drills where you start the drill by pushing against a short backspin, and then continue the drill/rally with other shots. You won't get as much repetitive practice this way, but you'll practice what you need to develop. For example, your partner serves short to your forehand; you push quick off the bounce to your partner's backhand; he pushes quick to your backhand; and you loop, either forehand or backhand. (Or, alternately, your partner loops off your forehand push, if it's "his" drill – and you still get practice pushing!)

Meanwhile, a nice drill is to push forehand to forehand (or backhand to backhand) where both players push short – but the first time a player pushes long (by mistake), you loop. This develops your short push, develops your loop, and best of all, it develops your judgment on whether a ball is long or short.

April 11, 2016 – How to Do Demonstrations
[Note – this isn't about improving your game, but it is about improving your demonstrations!]

Suppose you have a large gathering and you are asked to do a demonstration/exhibition? Here are some pointers on how to do a *great* one.

1. **Bring needed equipment.** Besides the obvious table and balls, you might want to have spare rackets for players from the audience, barriers, boxes of balls (to demonstrate multiball), ball pickup nets, and a scoreboard. You might also want to bring any props you might use – mini- or over-sized rackets, for example. Bring flyers about local table tennis events, especially coaching programs if it's for kids.
2. **Introduce yourself and your partner.** Then give a short talk about the sport. Keep it short – you don't want to bore them. I typically ask them (with a show of hands) how many have played table tennis before; have been to a table tennis club; own their

own racket; knew that table tennis was an Olympic sport; and knew that the best players train 6-8 hours/day and make over a million dollars per year. By asking for a show of hands, you get audience participation, which you want. I often end some of the questions with showing of hands of those too embarrassed to raise their hand either time (and I often slyly raise my hand). If you aren't good at public speaking, *practice!!!* When I first became a coach and had to lecture to groups, I took a class on public speaking, and spent hours practicing by talking to my dog and the dryer. (It makes it more realistic if you have something alive or moving to practice in front of.)

3. **Make sure to talk about local table tennis opportunities!** Here's a good time to give out flyers.

4. **Give a short demo** – again, keep it short. Make sure to have a partner who can rally with you. Then demo the forehand, the backhand, looping, and lobbing, giving a short explanation for each. You can also do chopping if one of you can do that and the other can attack them consistently. You can also give a short demo on serves, showing how a backspin ball can come back into the net, for example. Let it be known that at the end you'll let them try to return the serves.

5. **Do an exhibition.** It's not a real game; you want spectacular rallies. I like to start by telling the audience that a terrible thing has happened, that my partner – after years of getting coaching from me – has gotten a big head, and thinks he/she can beat *me*. Then we have a challenge match to 11 points. Neither of us use our spin serves, though I'll throw in a lot of spectacular high-toss serves and maybe a few fast ones, but nothing deceptive. Then rally! Lobbing is best, but don't overdo it or it gets a bit redundant – and perhaps save the best lobbing points for toward the end. (I often fall to the ground and lob while lying and sitting on the floor.) You can play the exhibition "straight," with just good shots, or do more humorous trick shots, as I often like to do, where I pull out the big racket, the mini-racket, a clipboard, do 50-foot serves, blow the ball back, and argue with the umpire.

6. **Finish with audience participation.** I find the best way is to let

the audience line up and try to return serves – two misses and they are out (and they'll usually race to the end of the line to try again). Be flamboyant – serve with sidespin, put your racket on the table, and move to where the ball should go and catch it. Or serve backspin, and as you do so, call out, "Don't hit into the net!" I often ask if they want "Speed or Spin," and then give it to them. After you've done this a few rounds, that's the time to explain how to return spins serves, and then take your time with each player, showing them where to aim – down and to the side against sidespin, and up against backspin.

7. **Give a final short statement**, reminding them about local table tennis events, and thank them for coming.

YOUR GAME

December 29, 2016 – What Are Your Main Weapons?

What are the best weapons in your game, or in the game that you want to develop? Think this over, and perhaps write them down. Then consider this: How do you get these weapons into play? How do you follow-up these weapons to make sure you win the point?

If your best weapon is a put-way shot, then you need ways to set up this shot. If your best weapon is a rallying shot, then you need ways to force these types of rallies. If your best weapon is your serve, then you need ways to follow it up, or the serve is wasted. (If you rely on the opponent outright missing against your serve or popping it up over and over, then you are facing weaker players and need to aim for higher competition.)

Some players have one overpowering strength that they rely on, such as a big forehand loop. But a big forehand loop doesn't help a lot if you don't have serves, receives, and rallying shots to set it up, and the footwork to get into position for it. Some have multiple strengths, such as a serve and attack, making their game twice as deadly. Decide what yours are (or should be), and develop them into deadly weapons that you set up, use, and follow up on over and over.

Ideally, develop three types of overpowering strengths: serve and receive (which start every rally); rallying shots; and attacking/put-away shots. Then go out and terrorize opponents with your triple-threat weapons!

October 31, 2016 – How Do You Win and Lose Points?

Most players only have a vague idea of how they win and lose points. Ask them how they won or lost most points, and they really don't know. They just have a general idea of their playing style or game plan, and don't really get any feedback on its success, i.e. what is working and what is not.

Top players who have played many years generally get a good feeling for this, though not always. But if you want to become a top player, you need to develop this sense of what works and what does not. How do you do that?

Videotape yourself playing a few matches. Then watch the video, and keep track of how each point was won or lost, from your perspective. (You can also have a coach do this for you.) Did you win it with your serve (receiver missed it or popped it up), with serve and attack (serve set you up for an attack, though not an easy winner), receive, forehand or backhand loop, forehand or backhand drive, blocking, placement, consistency, pushing, lobbing, or what? Make a chart and keep track, adding columns for each type of thing that wins a point for you as they come up. Also keep track of how many points you won with different serves and receives.

When you've done this, you might have a better idea of what works and doesn't work, and with that feedback, you can both develop your game to focus on what works, develop the parts that aren't working, and get a better feel in match play for what is tactically working or not working.

May 12, 2014 – Anyone Can Become Very Good at Something

It's hard to be great at something. Often it's said that it takes about 10,000 hours to become truly great at something – and that's not just putting in the hours, that's working hard. (The "10,000 hour rule" is mentioned repeatedly in some books and articles, such as "Outliers." It's not a strict rule, just a rough guideline) While we can debate on just how long it really takes to be truly great, and find all sorts of exceptions in both directions, it is a good approximation of what it takes, whether it's in sports, arts, academics, or most other fields.

The problem is that 10,000 hours takes 10,000 hours. Most people have jobs or school, and other obligations such as family, etc., and can't devote their lives to this. Suppose you do three times a week for two hours. Then it's going to take 33 years to get to 10,000 hours! The problem in table tennis is by that time you'll probably be past your physical peak. More importantly, if you take 33 years to get to those 10,000 hours, most of those 10,000 hours are wasted as you forget much of the early training, i.e. 10,000 hours over 33 years isn't the same as 10,000 hours in ten years (i.e. about 20 hours/week). It needs to be a bit more condensed.

What does this mean for you, the average player who can't put in 20 hours a week for a decade? It means you probably aren't going to be world champion, or even seriously challenge the players who compete to be world champion. It's a bitter pill to swallow, but someone has to tell you the truth.

But guess what? Anyone can become *very good* at something, and it doesn't take anywhere close to 10,000 hours in ten years. Pick out the aspects of table tennis where you can be good, and develop your game around that. It may take 10,000 hours to develop a truly world-class game, but it doesn't take that long to develop a very good serve, or a very good loop against backspin, a very good block, or any other specific aspect of your game. They key is to develop it properly, watching how the top players do it, perhaps working with a coach, and focus on developing it until it is very good. You can probably do that in 100 hours. (My serves are considered very good by most standards. I developed them mostly be practicing them 20 minutes a day, five days a week, for about a year. That's a little over 80 hours total.)

Here's the double pay-off. If you develop one aspect of your game, other parts will follow. If you develop a very good serve, then you get lots of follow-up shots, and so you develop a very good attack. If you develop a very good loop against backspin, you'll get a lot of blocked returns, and you'll develop a very good follow-up to your opening loop. If you develop a very good block, you'll develop ways to win points that way, either with put-away shots after you've blocked your opponent out of position and forced a weak shot, or numerous other ways – more aggressive blocks, change-of pace blocks, pure steadiness, etc. And so on. (The three examples I give here are ones I myself went through.)

And here's the triple pay-off. When parts of your game become very good, your overall level will tend to go up, and you'll end up playing better players – and they'll force you to raise your level to an even higher standard. So becoming very good at one shot often improves other aspects of your game, and brings up your whole level. One key here is to understand the whole process. Developing one shot doesn't mean it ends with just developing that shot – the end is to both developing that shot and the other techniques that go with that shot, i.e. setting it up and following it up.

So what are you waiting for? If a "pro" has to put in 10,000 hours, can you do 1% of that, and put in 100 hours to develop one aspect until it's very good, knowing the double and triple pay-offs that will follow? Go to it.

August 29, 2016 – Keep a Notebook

Do you keep a table tennis notebook? I did for years, and I recommend you do as well. I used a steno notebook. From front to back, I would take notes on my own game – what I was working on, what drills I was doing, what worked and didn't work in matches, etc. On the other side – back to front – I kept tactical notes on opponents. When the side on me was filled up (it usually went first), I'd get a new notebook for my game and start fresh. At tournaments, I'd bring past notebooks (with the ever-growing notes on opponents), and would be ready against any opponent I'd ever played against.

After doing this for perhaps a decade, I realized that I'd been doing it so long that notes about opponents I'd played were all in my head, and that I no longer needed to consult my notes to remember them – but the very act of writing them down made it easier to remember. I eventually retired my notebook in regard to tactical notes against opponents – though I sometimes would write down the notes as a memory aid, and then put them aside – but for years afterwards I kept notes on my own development and what I needed to do to improve.

These days you might use a smart phone for such notes, or go old school with a steno notebook. It still works!

While I no longer have a notebook for my game, I still keep notes on regular opponents of players I coach, which I jot down at tournaments and later type up in my coaching files on my computer. When I show up at major tournaments I bring these top secret printouts.

December 28, 2015 – You're Your Yore

Every part of your game has a history. If you are a longtime player, you should be able to look at any serve or stroke in your game and remember its history – how it started, how it developed, and where it stands today. If you are a more recent player, it's even easier as it's all fresh in your mind since you've just started.

The key thing to remember is that your history changes constantly; you are in control of it. Why not take an inventory of your game – all of it – and think about how it got to be where it is, and then, more importantly, think about where it should be. Then begin the history that'll lead to it being where it should be. Develop your yore.

Suppose your pushes are consistent, but not very heavy. Why aren't they heavy? Because you have a history of not pushing heavy, and every time you don't push heavy, you re-enforce the nonheaviness habit of your pushes. So work on pushing heavy, begin to do it, and eventually you'll have a history of pushing heavy – and it'll be where it should be. And then you'll be able to look back at the history of your push, and note that moment in time when you began to create a history of pushing heavy, and so developed that as part of your game.

Every aspect of your game has a history, and you have control over developing the history that leads to each aspect. Take control of this history and develop your game to where it should be. You're your yore.

May 18, 2015 – Become a Player of Routine

Nearly all top athletes are creatures of ritual. This isn't superstition; it's a way for them to systematically be at their best. This includes finding little ways to always be at their best physically, mentally, tactically, and equipmentally. (Yes, I just coined that term.)

- **Physically**, this means preparing for play the same way each time.

This includes getting enough sleep with regular hours; eating properly (and a lot if you train a lot); hydration; and proper warm-up. Warming up isn't just at the table; it means doing, for example, some easy jogging and stretching before play to get the body ready. Once at the table, it means going through a systematic practice routine that allows you to warm up and tune up all of your major techniques. It also means having snacks and drinks ready during a session.

- **Mentally**, this means preparing yourself so your mind is at its best for play. This is probably the most overlooked area. Nearly all top athletes have a routine for this. For example, many listen to music, often a specific song or musician, which gets them mentally ready. Others meditate to clear their minds. Most top players develop little rituals at the table as well, perhaps tapping the table with their hands or bouncing the ball a certain number of times before serving. Everyone needs to find their own way of doing this.

- **Tactically**, this means going over the tactics of the upcoming match (assuming you are about to play games). If you know the opponent (either from playing, watching, or scouting him), then you should decide what the most important things to remember should be, and usually get it down to a few simple items, such as 2-3 serves, 1-2 receives, and 1-2 rallying tactics. (This is slightly more than what a coach should tell you, but you should be able to deal with a few more things on your own, since you are choosing them.) Above all, remind yourself to stop and think about these things periodically during the match to make sure you are actually executing the needed tactics. The tactics should be flexible, and change as needed, but you should make a habit of always having a rough plan. If you don't know the opponent, then your tactics should focus on what you want to do, and adjust as you learn how your opponent plays – which shouldn't take long.

- **Equipmentally**, this means having the proper equipment on hand. There's the obvious: your racket, covering, and shoes. Make sure they are in good condition. Then there's the less obvious: backup rackets, towels (especially if it's humid), and a wet cloth or paper towel to step on between points if the floors are slippery. Make a habit of making sure you have everything present and ready.

January 12, 2015 – Develop Your Primary and Secondary Skills

To play at any level you have to have something you can use to win points at that level. Typically this means a big forehand or backhand, tricky serves, a strong counter-hitting or blocking game, or perhaps defensive skills such as chopping. These are a player's point-winning skills, which might be called his primary skills.

But there are also secondary skills which set up the point-winning skills. Having a big forehand loop, for example, doesn't always help if you don't have ways to set it up via these secondary skills, such as a good serve, a good receive, a spinny opening loop, a good backhand, or just fast footwork to get you into position in a rally for the big loop.

Serves can be both a primary point-winning skill or a secondary set-up one. Players with big breaking spin serves (often long) often use them as a point-winning skill, either winning the point outright or setting up such a weak return that it essentially wins the point outright. Others have simpler-looking serves that are usually short and low, with varied spin (often backspin or no-spin that looks like backspin), that force defensive returns that might not win the point directly, but consistently set up a primary attack, usually a strong opening loop. (Receivers will generally make fewer outright mistakes against such short serves that don't have the big spinny break of a deeper serve, but because the serves are short and because they aren't always sure of the spin at first they tend to receive passively.)

Often a player seems to have a primary point-winning skill when in fact his strength is a secondary skill that sets up a point-winning one – and the point-winning one simply seems strong because he gets so many weak returns to use it against. But against stronger players, whose returns aren't as weak, the primary skill might not be so strong. These players can improve dramatically by improving the point-winning skill. Similarly, players with big point-winning skills might fall apart against stronger players who don't give them the big point-winning shot so easily. These players can improve dramatically by improving their secondary set-up skills.

Developing secondary set-up skills has a huge additional advantage. They set the player up to attack over and over, resulting in lots and lots of attacking practice, i.e. point-winning skills, and so those primary point-winning skills improve dramatically. That's why developing good set-up serves, for example, will lead to lots of attack practice and thereby a much improved attack, leading to a higher level of play.

Examine your game and decide what your strengths are. If they are primary point-winning skills, then perhaps focus on developing secondary skills to set up these point-winning skills. If they are secondary set-up skills, then perhaps focus on developing primary skills to win the point. Often players get stuck at a level because they are missing one of these types of skills.

December 25, 2016 – Maximize Coverage For Your Stronger Side

Whether you are stronger on the forehand or backhand, you should maximize coverage with your stronger side. Ideally, you'll be equally strong on both sides, but that is rare. At the very least, most players are stronger on one side in some situations – for example, better on the backhand in fast rallies, better on the forehand when attacking against slower shots.

And yet many players do not maximize the coverage of their stronger side. Analyze your game, and decide which side is your stronger side in any given situation. For example, many top players receive short serves better with their backhand, usually with a banana flip. So when they see a short serve coming, they often step over and receive with their backhands, even from the forehand corner. Others may have very strong rallying backhands, and so might cover over half the table with their backhands. Or (more commonly at the higher levels) they might be stronger on the forehand, and so cover more of the table with that.

So start training to use your stronger side to cover more of the table in given situations – because using a stronger shot to cover more of the table makes you a stronger player!

March 14, 2016 – Outlining the Book on Your Game

I once wrote, "If you can't write a book on your game, either you don't know your game or you don't have a game." It's as simple as that.

You don't need to actually write that book, but you should outline it. This will force you think about the various aspects of your game – your strengths, weaknesses, and everything in between, as well as where you want to go with your game. It'll get you to actually thinking about the things you should be thinking about if you want to improve. So let's put together an outline of such an outline. Note that we're not interested in inventorying and analyzing every stroke; what's important are what techniques you actually use. Your assignment, should you choose to accept, is to complete this outline for your game.

1. **General**
   a. What is your style of play in one sentence? (It can be a long one.)
      i. Example – the author's: All-out forehand attacker, both looping and smashing (but first loop sometimes too soft), with strong serve & attack, good receive, a steady but too passive backhand, and steady, all-around defense – blocking, fishing, lobbing, and sometimes even chopping.
   b. Strengths
      i. What's the strongest part of your game?
      ii. How do you get it into play?
      iii. How are you turning this strength into something that can dominate even against stronger players?
   c. Weaknesses
      i. What's the weakest part of your game?
      ii. How do cover for it?
      iii. What are you doing to improve this weakness?

2. **Strokes**
   a. Forehand attack
      i. Against push
      ii. Against block
      iii. Against loop (counterloop or smash)
   b. Forehand defense or counter-attack
   c. Backhand attack
      i. Against push
      ii. Against block
      iii. Against loop (counterloop or smash)
   d. Backhand defense or counter-attack
   e. Pushing
      i. Long
      ii. Short

3. **Footwork**

a. Close to table
b. Off table
c. In and out during rally
d. Covering middle
e. Short to forehand and back
f. Recovery
g. General positioning
h. Ready position

4. **Serve**
   a. Serves that set up your attack
   b. Trick serves (important, but not to be overused)
   c. Variety of motions
   d. Variety of spins
   e. Fast, deep serves
   f. Variety of depths and depth control
   g. Low to net

5. **Receive**
   a. Forehand against long serves
   b. Backhand against long serves
   c. Forehand against short serves
      i. Short push
      ii. Long push
      iii. Flip
      iv. Variation
   d. Backhand against short serves
      i. Short push
      ii. Long push
      iii. Flip
      iv. Variation

6. **Physical**
   a. General fitness
   b. Foot speed
   c. Strength
   d. Loose, relaxed muscles
   e. Endurance

7. **Mental**

     a. Clear-minded and focused
         i. At start of match
        ii. When behind
       iii. When ahead
       iv. At end of close games
     b. Know how to recover from loss of focus
     c. Know when to call time-outs to recover focus

8. **Tactical**
     a. Understand what serves set up your game
     b. Understand what receives set up your game
     c. Understand what type of rallies you want to get into
     d. Know how to get your strengths into play
     e. Know how to cover for your weaknesses
     f. Good at scouting opponents in advance
     g. Good at analyzing opponents during a match
     h. Consistently able to find two or three simple tactics that allow you to win
     i. Understand what you need to develop in your game to increase your tactical arsenal

PRACTICE

October 26, 2015 – Develop a Practice Partner

It's the lament of developing players everywhere: How do I get a good practice partner? You might get lucky and find someone at your local club who happens to be about the same level, has the same burning desire to improve, and is both willing and available to train at the same times and number of hours that you want to do so. If so, you've hit the jackpot, and your game will be going places.

But more often finding someone who meets all this criteria is difficult. So you may have to go to option two – develop a practice partner by practicing with a weaker player.

This enhances your chances in multiple ways. First, the number of players below your level is almost for certain far greater than the number of players right around your level, and so the chances are greater of finding a compatible partner. Second, because it gives a weaker player the opportunity to train with someone stronger, the incentive is greater, so you are more likely to find a willing partner. And third, it will likely force you to focus on your basics, i.e. re-enforce the foundation of your game, which is so often overlooked.

Let's elaborate on that last point. Many players look for practice partners at their level or higher, who can push them to a higher level. This often means playing faster and faster, which should make you better – and there's some truth to that. But what's often missing is the consistency part. If you ask a beginner and most intermediate players what the biggest difference between an average player and a top player, they would most likely say the pace they play at. If you ask a top player the same question, he'd likely say consistency. By hitting with a weaker player, you are forced to slow down a bit and focus on consistency – and that should be the foundation of your game.

How do you develop such a practice partner out of a weaker player? At the start you have to be patient as the player won't be able to play at either your pace or consistency. So you use your powers as the stronger player and focus on consistency as well as accuracy – keep the ball right to their forehand and backhand pockets, so they can fine-tune their strokes and develop their consistency. And a magical thing will happen –not only will they improve, but they will get more and more used to your shots, and soon they will be practicing with you on an almost even basis. (I've not only done this in the past with several practice partners, I've seen others do it many times.)

And note that they will be improving not because you are pushing them to play faster and faster, but because both of you are focused on consistency. Only increase the pace when both players are consistent at a given pace. (This is also a hint about practicing with *any* player – focus on consistency. Stronger players play faster because they are *consistent* at that speed.)

So if you are having trouble finding a good practice partner, change your mind-set and develop one, and together you can take the table tennis world by storm.

September 12, 2016 – The More Two Players Drill Together the Better They Drill Together

One of the keys to improving is getting a good practice partner. Usually these are two players who are roughly the same level. But it's more important that they both want to improve, are willing to work together, and are available to train on a regular basis. The more they train together the more used to each other they get, and the better each plays in these drills. This leads to both players' levels escalating up – an upward spiral to excellence!

I want to emphasize how much better you play when you drill with someone regularly – you get used to their shots, and your own shots become more and more natural and consistent, as well as more powerful. Some might think this is artificial, since you are playing against the same player and shots, which isn't what happens in tournaments or leagues. But the key is how much this type of drilling develops your foundation. (This doesn't mean you only practice with one player, but if you are able to practice with multiple players, the more you hit with them the better you'll drill with them.)

Players still need to practice with and play others with different styles, especially matches – that's imperative – but drilling with a good partner (or partners) develops the foundation that's so important to developing your game.

Once you find someone to train with regularly, take turns with the drills. But remember that in any drill, *both* players are doing the drill. If one player is doing a footwork drill to the other's block, then the other is doing a blocking drill. Players not only need to learn to move and attack, but also to control an opponent's shots. And remember even blocking is a footwork drill – you need to step to the ball, not just reach.

Don't forget to get a box of balls and do some multiball training! Multiball training makes up about 1/3 of the training of world-class players.

April 18, 2016 – Shot Awareness in Practice

What you do in practice you will do in matches. Therefore, you should be aware of the placement of your shots in practice drills, both direction and depth. This gives you feedback on your accuracy so you can make adjustments. Without this feedback you can't really improve your ball control and improve your accuracy.

When you play a match, your attacks and blocks should normally go deep to the wide corners or the opponent's middle (roughly playing elbow). Long pushes should also go very deep, mostly to the corners. When I tell players to do this, they often say that they are just trying to get the ball on the table, and that they can't control it well enough to really aim for these spots. *Exactly!!!* But if you do this in practice, your shots will become more accurate, you will be able to go to these three spots, and it will become a habit. But only if you become aware of your shots in practice so that you can make constant adjustments as you strive for better accuracy.

June 22, 2015 – Conquer the One-Winged Blues by Developing Your Weaker Side

Many players are much stronger on one side than the other. Often this is the forehand, but not always. They generally find tactical ways through serve, receive, and placement to cover for their weaker side while trying to dominate with their stronger side. This often works, to a point. However, it means accepting an inherent weakness in one's game, which often becomes a barrier to improvement.

Slightly stronger players – the ones you are trying to learn to compete with – will usually have the tools and tactical skills to play into this weakness. For example, if you have a strong forehand but weaker backhand, a smart opponent will simply serve fast and deep to the backhand, and hit fast, quick rally shots there, with the threat of a fast serve or shot to the forehand if you try to cover the backhand with the forehand. Or he might serve short to the forehand, drawing you in over the table, and then go deep to the backhand. Or he might just serve deep to the forehand and quick-block your return to the backhand. There are many ways of finding the weak side.

Suppose you are stronger on one side. Much of this might be because of your grip, playing stance, or just your mental mode, where you focus on the strong side (for example, are stuck in "forehand mode"), and so get caught on the weak side. But these are relatively easy things to fix, if you know what you are doing. (If you don't, get a coach or consult with a knowledgeable player.) Spend some time developing that "weaker" side so that when you are forced to use it, it's pretty strong, even if not as good as your stronger side. It might be as simple as learning to mentally change from "forehand mode" to "two-winged mode," or even "backhand mode." Or it might mean small changes in your grip or stance.

What you want to do is to dominate many points with your strong side when you can, but also force your opponent to sacrifice his own normal tactics, forcing him to instead use his tactics to find your "weaker" side. To do so he'll have to adjust his tactics and game, which puts him at a disadvantage until he actually gets to the weaker side, which essentially means he's willing to give up points in return for doing so. And then, when he finds it, you want him to find that weak side isn't so weak, and that even after giving up points to get to it, he still has a difficult struggle to score.

And so he'll be stuck trying to decide whether it's worth giving up points to find your "weak" side, which isn't so weak, or give up on the tactics that avoided your "strong" side – and so you'll be able to play your strong side more often. It gives him a no-win tactical choice. Isn't that a wonderful thing?

February 23, 2015 – Shadow Practice When You Miss

Table tennis is a game of technique, timing, and adjustment. When you miss a shot, that means something went wrong with your technique or timing. That means something went wrong with your muscle memory, which includes both the technique and timing. So, what should you do to get back and reinforce that muscle memory?

You shadow practice the shot. Immediately after missing, before whatever went wrong has a chance to become part of your muscle memory, do it the *right* way. Imagine the same incoming ball you just missed against, including its speed, spin, and location. Then shadow practice the shot the way you should have done it, and visualize the ball doing what it was supposed to do, i.e. the perfect shot. This is how you reinforce the correct muscle memory. Put the feel of the miss out of your memory; thinking about it only reinforces in your muscle memory something you don't want reinforced.

This is especially important for beginning and intermediate players, whose muscle memory is not as developed, but advanced players should do this as well to re-enforce the proper muscle memory. Ultimately, this is the goal of the constant practice needed to become a top player – the primary purpose is to develop and reinforce those muscle memories so they'll remember to come out when needed in a match.

PRACTICE MATCHES

October 17, 2016 – Play Both Weaker and Stronger Players

Many players who want to improve make the mistake of trying to play mostly stronger players. The result is the opponent controls play, and all the player can do is react to the stronger player's shots, or go for wild shots. A player may develop some shots this way, but it'll be hard to develop new shots or to learn how to use them in a game situation.

If you are trying to improve you need to both try out new shots that you are developing and to try out new combinations and strategies. If you do this against a stronger player, you probably won't do so well, and you'll probably stop doing it. You won't have any way of knowing if the new shot, combination or strategy may work since the stronger player may win the point simply by being a stronger player against something you are just trying out and are not yet comfortable with.

Instead, try out new things against players who are weaker than you. Develop them against these players, in an environment where you can control play a little more (since you are the stronger player), and where you can see if the new things might work. Don't worry about winning or losing – this is practice – as you will undoubtedly lose sometimes when trying out something new, even against a weaker player. (Imagine how bad you'd lose in this case against a stronger player!) When your new techniques begin to work against a weaker player, then it's time to try them out against your peers and stronger players.

Example: suppose you want to develop your loop against backspin. The best way to do this is to serve backspin, and loop the pushed return. A stronger player may flip the serve, push short, quick push to a corner, or push extremely heavy – and you won't be able to develop the shot very well. A weaker player would be more likely to give you a ball that you can loop, which is what you need until the shot is more developed. You need to both develop the shot and your instincts on when to use it, how to follow it up, etc. When you can do it against a weaker player, then it's time to try it out against tougher competition.

Everyone wants to play against stronger players, and you do need to play stronger players so they can push you to play at a higher level. But often it helps to play weaker players so you can develop the weapons you'll want to use against those stronger players.

September 29, 2014 – Improvised Games

Many players improve by using practice drills that mimic something they need to improve on in matches. But why not turn that around, and play matches that mimic something you need to improve on in matches? It's not redundant – it's a matter of playing Improvised Games instead of regular ones.

For example, play a game or match where you always serve short backspin to the opponent's backhand, he pushes deep to your backhand, you backhand loop, and then you play out the point. Keep score like a regular game, and do your best to win under the improvised rules.

On the following page are ten Improvised Games you might try out. But don't restrict yourself to these. Look at your own game, figure out what you need to work on, and design Improvised Games that allow you to work on those techniques. (POP = Play Out Point.)

<u>**Improvised Games to Improve Your Game**</u>
1. Serve short backspin to opponent's backhand; he pushes to your backhand; you backhand loop; POP. Alternate versions: Your first

backhand loop goes to a specified location, then POP. Or take it one step further, and opponent's first block goes to a specified location. For example, you backhand loop to his backhand, he blocks to your forehand, and then POP. You can also vary the short serve with no-spin serves.

2. Same as #1, except opponent pushes serve to your forehand, and you loop the forehand, and then POP. Or use alternate versions, as explained in #1. You can also have opponent push to your backhand and you forehand loop, if you have good footwork.

3. Serve short side-top to forehand or backhand. Opponent flips either anywhere, or to pre-arranged spot. You attack, POP.

4. Serve varied long serves to opponent's backhand. Opponent soft loops serve back. You attack, POP.

5. Put a box or towel near the middle of the table, cutting off perhaps half the table. Play a backhand-to-backhand game where the server starts the rally by serving topspin. Or do a variation where it's forehand to forehand, or forehand to backhand. Or variations where one player loops, the other blocks. The goal here isn't just to win the point, but to play great rallies that'll carry over into real matches.

6. Need to work on your pushing? Play a pushing game where both players can only push, with rallies starting with a backspin serve. But since most players push better on the backhand, there might be a tendency to push to the forehand in this game, since the opponent isn't allowed to attack. So set a rule where you can never push twice in a row to the forehand. Or set a rule where players can attack, but if they do they have to win the point on one shot.

7. To work on serve and attack, play a game where the server has only two shots to win the point, not including the serve. Or, as long as you don't get into the habit of trying to rip every ball, play only one shot after the serve.

8. For very fast forehand-oriented players, play a game where you can only play forehand shots. Or perhaps you can only play one backhand in a row. (This is one of my favorites, but it's gotten harder as I've gotten older.)

9. To work on short pushes, play a game where each player serves short backspin and then both players continue the rally pushing every ball short (i.e. given the chance the ball would bounce twice). If either player thinks the ball is going long he lets it go, and if it goes long he wins the point; if it bounces twice he loses the point. An alternate version is where players can attack, but if they do they must win the point on one shot.

10. Play a lobbing, fishing, or chopping game to work on your defense, where you aren't allowed to attack. Alternate version is where you can attack, but must win the point on one shot if you do.

December 30, 2016 – How to Play Practice Matches with a Weaker Player

When playing practice matches with much weaker players, here are two suggestions: 1) Simplify your serves so you get higher quality returns to practice against; and 2) Decide something specific you want to work on, such as forehand loop, and use your higher level technique to force rallies where you can work on those shots. For example, serve short backspin and attack any long return with your forehand. If you need blocking practice, push long to them, and block. And so on.

At the same time, you should fight to win every one of these points, given the conditions above. You can practice mental focus and hustle against any level of player. You might also want to play some matches against weaker players where you ignore the above two suggestions, just to work on your "win every point" skills, including serves and using your best game, not just what you need to work on. (You might want to do this especially before a big tournament, to focus on your general match playing skills.) Some might argue you should play every match this way, even against much weaker players, but I think you lose an opportunity to practice certain things if you do that all the time.

DRILLS

February 8, 2016 – Looping Against Backspin Drills

It's easy practicing topspin rallies since you can do them over and over in the same rally. The same is not true for practicing against backspin, unless you happen to have a chopper to practice with – and that's not quite the same either, since a chop against topspin comes out differently than a push, and you don't get practice switching from playing against backspin to playing against topspin or block. So how should you get your practice against backspin? There's a three-step process.

1. **Multiball.** Here's where you learn and hone the forehand and backhand loops. You can do this with a coach or a practice partner where you take turns.
2. **Serve and Loop Drills.** You serve backspin (usually short), and partner pushes it back long so you can practice looping. In each case you should play out the point. There are four main variations of this given below, in progressing difficulty. In all four of these variations you should probably do your first loop to the same

spot each time so you can start off each drill with your partner making a good block. You might also arrange so your partner's first block goes to the same spot, depending on your level. For example, your first loop might go to your partner's backhand, he blocks to your forehand, and then you play out the point. There are many variations of these drills; decide what you need to work on and design the drill around that.

    a. Partner pushes to one spot, such as wide forehand or wide backhand, and you forehand or backhand loop, then play out the point.

    b. Partner pushes to wide forehand or middle and you forehand loop, or partner pushes to wide backhand or middle backhand and you backhand loop. While you know in advance whether you'll be doing a forehand or backhand loop, you now have to move to do so. Note that you should generally cover more of the table with the forehand (where the body is not in the way so you have more range, plus it's usually more powerful), which is why the backhand drill covers less of the table. But if you prefer backhand looping from the middle, make that adjustment. If you are a forehand player who covers a lot of ground with the forehand, then have your partner push to 2/3 of the table, or even the whole table, and you follow with a forehand.

    c. Partner pushes to either wide forehand or wide backhand and you have to react with either a forehand or backhand loop. Partner should practice deceptive pushing starting here – sometimes aiming one way, then going the other direction, and try pushing quick off the bounce.

    d. Partner pushes anywhere randomly and you have to react with either a forehand or backhand loop. Again, partner should sometimes aim one way and then go the other way, quick off the bounce.

3. **Improvised Games**. Do the very same drills you did in the Serve and Loop Drills, except now you should play games that start out in these ways. Keeping score makes sure both players fight hard,

and very closely resemble real game situations. Choose what's needed for you. At the advanced levels mostly use the variation where your partner pushes the serve back anywhere and you loop, and then play out the point.

February 15, 2016 – Improving Side-to-Side Reaction

Many players develop pretty good strokes, timing, and footwork, and in practice drills, where they know where the ball is going (i.e. rote drills), can execute them pretty well. But once they get into a more random drill or game, where they don't know where the ball is going (i.e. forehand or backhand), they fall apart. How can you fix this problem?

The key thing here is reaction. Once you have good strokes, you can do various random drills such as having your partner or coach randomly block to all parts of the table while you loop or drive them back to the same spot, or serve backspin that your partner or coach pushes back anywhere and you have to loop. (Focus on a good neutral position, react rather than trying to anticipate, and *step* to the ball.) These are excellent drills. But many players struggle with them, and don't get enough practice time on these types of drills to progress as fast as they'd like.

There's a simple alternative. Find someone who can help you out – it doesn't have to be a table tennis player, it can be a friend, spouse, son/daughter, *anyone* – and simply have them randomly point left or right. You react by shadow-stroking either a forehand or backhand, depending on which way they point. Or, if you want to get fancy (and more closely mimic a game situation), have them toss balls at you randomly, forehand or backhand, and you react, either by shadow-stroking, or actually hitting them with your racket. (It's basically multiball, except since they are tossing the ball at you instead of hitting off a racket, anyone can do it.) In both cases, it's not exactly the same since you aren't reacting to a ball coming off a paddle, but it's reasonably close.

Then watch as your apparent reaction time in game-type play improves! It's all about zeroing in on a weakness, and practicing the specific thing that you are having trouble with. The principle applies here and in all other aspects of table tennis . . . and life.

May 26, 2014 – Random Drills

One of the best ways to improve is through multiball training, and one of the best drills you can do there (besides an intense stroke workout) are random drills. When you play a match, you don't know where your opponent is going to put the ball, so you have to be ready to cover the whole table.

A beginner or anyone working to develop their strokes should mostly do rote drills, where the player knows where the ball is going each time so they can focus on the stroke itself. At the advanced levels they still do rote drills, but mostly to tune the strokes and develop faster and faster footwork. As players develop, and especially at higher levels, players do more and more random drills. This allows them to develop the nearly instant reactions to incoming shots that they will face in a match.

You could, of course, just play matches, which is the ultimate random drill. But while that's important, you also want to focus on specific shots to react to. For example, if you want to react to whether a fast incoming ball goes to your forehand or backhand, you can get limited practice with this in a game, with perhaps two or three shots per rally, and then go pick up the ball. Or you could have a coach feed continuous multiball, and you get maybe twenty times the practice on this in the same amount of time.

A problem with random drills is that you can't really do them very well live (i.e. with a practice partner) until both players are relatively advanced. And so players generally don't do them until they are somewhat proficient – and then they practically have to start from scratch doing random drills that they should have been doing early on. Once you can hit a decent forehand or backhand you should be doing some sort of random drills as well. Few do so.

So get a coach or a practice partner you can take turns with, and do random multiball drills. At first have them feed the ball randomly to two spots – middle forehand and middle backhand. Make sure your first move is the right one; you have more time than you think, so don't rush. When you are comfortable at doing this at rally speeds, then go random the whole table. Learn to cover all five spots – wide forehand, middle forehand, middle, middle backhand, and wide backhand.

Let me emphasize – the key is that the first move must be the right move. No moving to the forehand and then changing when you see the ball going to the backhand, or vice versa.

Once you can do this proficiently in multiball, you should practice it live. Ideally you would at first do this with a coach or top player, who can control the ball well and keep the rallies going. But in most cases you'll need to do this with a practice partner who is more your own level. For this drill, you would play all of your shots to the same spot, either to your practice partner's backhand or forehand. As with multiball, start by having your partner hit randomly to just two spots (middle forehand or middle backhand), where you have to react properly to both shots and consistently drive the ball back to the pre-arranged spot. When you are proficient in this, then have your partner place the ball all over, in particular to the middle, which is often the hardest spot to cover.

When you are proficient at this drill in all its variations, and at speeds that approach match speeds, you will be able to do the same in a match, and your rallying ability and overall level will shoot up.

Here's a short video (26 seconds) of Soo Yeon Lee doing random multiball. She's hitting; depending on your level and playing style, you can do this hitting or looping.

www.facebook.com/101048626650453/videos/542672319154746

March 16, 2015 – To Play the Middle and Wide Corners You Have to Practice to Them

One of the most basic concepts in sports is that you must practice what you want to do in a match. The corollary to this is that what you do in practice is what you'll tend to do in a match. And yet, when it comes to ball placement, these are two of the most forgotten concepts in table tennis.

It's a basic tactical principle that most of your shots should go either to a wide angle – often outside the corners, to force your opponent to move and cover more ground – or at the opponent's middle, which is usually his playing elbow, the midpoint between his forehand and backhand, where he has to make a quick decision on whether to play a forehand or backhand, and then move into position. (There are also short balls, but that's a separate issue.) And so it's somewhat obvious that you'd want to practice putting balls to wide angles and to the middle, right? And yet, watch most practice drills, and you'll see that in the overwhelming majority of drills, players play to the corners, but no wider, and almost never to the middle. And so they are 1) not practicing what they want to do in a match, and 2) since what they do in practice is what they'll tend to do in a match, guess what they'll tend to do in a match?

So perhaps add two types of drills to your practice regimen. First, instead of drills where (for example) one player loops and other blocks, and it's all corner-to-corner, do this same drill, except both players go as wide as they comfortably can. The looper should try looping the ball *outside* the corner, often with hooking sidespin to go even wider. The blocker should take the ball quick off the bounce, which gives him the widest angle into the looper's forehand, and so he should block the ball as wide as possible. This doesn't mean going for risky extremes; it means going as wide as you *comfortably* can go. If you go too wide, you get less and less table, and will lose consistency.

You can do many similar drills. For example, when going backhand to backhand in a drill, why not focus on hitting balls a little bit outside the corners? There is an obvious advantage to going right at the corners, since it gives you more table and so it's safer, so you should find the right balance of when to go to the corner, and when to go for more angle.

Second, do drills where you go to the middle over and over. The most basic way is one player attacks the other's middle, while the other blocks from the middle, either forehand or backhand. The blocker can do this drill either by blocking with just forehand or just backhand over and over, or he can move back into a neutral position after each shot, and then react to the next shot with forehand or backhand. The result of such a drill? The attacker gets in the habit of attacking the middle, and so is able to do so in matches. The blocker practices something he will often see in matches — attacks to his middle — but rarely practices against, and so is rarely prepared for. And so both players improve their middle play.

So try out these drills, or come up with your own that allow you to practice placing the ball at wide angles and to the middle, perhaps by matching patterns you see in matches. And then do in matches what you do in practice!

May 9, 2014 – Why You Should Systematically Practice Receive

Many players spend lots of time systematically practicing their strokes and footwork. Each week they'll put in many hours practicing their forehand and backhand loops, drives, blocks, and all the other strokes in their repertoire. They'll practice their footwork. The smart and ambitious ones will even practice their serves, which often gives the most return on investment.

And yet most rely on matches to practice their serves. This doesn't make sense. If you can use matches as your primary way to develop a technique, then that would be the primary way players would develop all their shots. But any coach or experienced player will tell you that you need to develop these shots with systematic training. You do need match play or drills that simulate match play, but that's in addition to the systematic training needed to develop the shot itself.

So why do players rely on matches to develop their receive? My theory has always been that most players don't want to let rivals practice against their serves. Two players will gladly practice together, letting the opponent get used to all their shots, except for their serves. It's seems almost rude to ask a player to let you practice against their serves, since it seems as if you are practicing just to beat that player. And, unfortunately, there's some truth to this.

But it's also a huge handicap to players who cannot get past this idea of practicing receive only in matches. It's a two-way thing, but you have to find someone with varied serves who can serve to you over and over to develop your receive. Ideally, get a coach or top player, even if you have to pay them. Or find a peer, and both agree to let the other practice against their serves. Try to find someone who has a variety of serves.

And then practice against them. Practice attacking deep serves, usually with loops. Practice pushing short serves back long or short, and flipping them. Practice reading the varied spins. Practice against sidespins going in both directions, and against both topspin and backspin serves. Practice against every type of serve you might see in a match.

By doing this systematic training, your receive will improve dramatically. Since most of your peers won't be doing this type of training, you will soon leave them behind. And you'll rarely have to utter those infamous words heard so often, "I could have beaten him if I could return his serve."

April 6, 2015 – Tiger Woods Distraction Drill

It's always been strange to me how a problem faced by so many players is so rarely dealt with. And that is dealing with distractions. Over the years, how many matches have you lost because something distracted you and you lost your focus? What did you do to solve the problem?

Most likely you just tried to keep your focus in practice matches. That's like developing your loop only by looping in practice matches. It's part of the solution, but you'll develop it a lot faster by doing drills that allow you to focus on that one aspect of your game. Similarly, if you want to work on your focus, find drills that allow you to focus on that one aspect.

I'm going to give one example of how to work on this. When Tiger Woods was developing and practicing his strokes as an up-and-coming junior, his dad would sometimes jingle keys or do other distractions. Tiger learned to focus completely on what he was doing, and the result was nothing could cause him to lose his focus.

You can do the same. It may seem silly, but why not sometimes practice or play practice matches where someone does exactly that – jingles keys, plays distracting music or news, or just talks to you. Your job isn't to just ignore him; that's not the point. Your job is to tune him out so you don't really notice him, so that your entire focus is on what you are doing, like an absent-minded professor who doesn't notice his house is on fire. You need to be so focused and inside yourself that you truly don't pay attention to outside distractions. When you can do that, you'll never have a problem with distractions again.

CHAPTER SEVEN: SPORTS PSYCHOLOGY

November 21, 2016 – Getting "In the Zone" by Adapting to Your Opponent

Ever have a match where you were "In the Zone," where the ball seemed to slow down, and you could almost do no wrong? This is relative, of course; an intermediate player "In the Zone" isn't going to compete with a professional, but he would dominate against his normal peers. Here's a good article on the topic - Google "Being in the Zone – Sport's Holy Grail."

There are many articles and books about getting into this "Zone." (Dora Kurimay, a table tennis champion, can help with this, and another good one for this specifically is Michael Lardon's "Finding Your Zone" – he's also a former table tennis star.)

However, there's a pre-requisite to getting into the zone that has nothing to do with sports psychology. You cannot be "In the Zone" if you are not comfortable with what your opponent is doing. If your opponent does something that you are having trouble with, then you either have to keep him from doing it, or adapt to it. Being "In the Zone" means reacting automatically to what your opponent does, and you can't do that if you are uncomfortable with what he does.

Suppose your opponent has a weird inside-out forehand that looks like it's going one way, but goes the other. You can't really be in the zone against something like this if you are constantly going the wrong way. This means you have to adapt to what he's doing. Sometimes this means letting him do the shot simply so you can adjust to it. The more you see it, the more you adapt to it, and the more you can react to it. Once you are able to react to it properly, you are ready to be "In the Zone."

The worst thing you can do is to lose a match, and afterwards realize you never adapted to what the opponent was doing. This usually means you only faced it when you weren't ready for it, and so didn't adapt. Sometimes it's best to play right into it, so you know when it's coming, so you can make the adjustment.

Here's an example. Many years ago I had to play a 2200 long-pipped blocker, i.e. a "push-blocker," with no sponge under his long pips. Unfortunately, there was no one at my club who played like that or with that surface, and so it had been years since I'd played anything like it. Before the match I realized that if I didn't adapt to his no-sponge long pips, I could lose. But more importantly, I realized that *the only way I could lose* was if I didn't adapt to his long pips. Why? Because I knew that once I adapted to them, I would be "In the Zone," and he would have nothing to threaten me with. (He had very little attack.) So instead of playing to win points, right from the start all I did was rally into his long pips. We had lots of long rallies, and we battled close, but I didn't worry about the score until near the end of the game. Around 8-all, I went after his forehand and middle, and won three straight points. The second game was a repeat – again, lots of long rallies. Near the end of that game I figured it was time – and then I played to win the points. I was now completely comfortable against his pips, and I was now "In the Zone." I won easily the rest of the way.

There are many other examples. Does your opponent have a very strong backhand? Perhaps play into it intentionally a few points, challenging his strength as you adapt to it so that you'll be comfortable against it when you have to, and then go back to your game. Does he have a spinnier loop then you are used to? Play into it a few times so you can adapt to it, then go back to your game. Does he push heavier than you are used to? Serve backspin into it so you can attack a few so you can adapt. And so on. Sometimes you might challenge the strength and then go to the weakness. For example, after challenging the opponent's strong backhand so you can adapt to it, perhaps counter-attack to his weaker forehand side. You get the best of both worlds – you adapt to his strength, and you play into his weakness.

None of this means you should continue to let your opponent play his strengths – you should normally use tactics to avoid them. But if you are going to have to face them, then it's better to adapt to them than not to do so, and adapting to them allows you to enter "The

Zone." Suddenly his strengths, when he gets to play them, won't be so scary.

So next time you have a match, quickly find out what your opponent does that gives you trouble, and do what it takes to adapt to it. Then play your best game, where you now can be "In the Zone" against whatever your opponent throws at you.

October 13, 2014 – Working With Your Subconscious

The single most important thing to understand about table tennis training is that *you are training your subconscious to automatically perform each technique properly*. When you do a shot, you don't consciously move your feet into the exact proper position; decide what shot to do and where and how hard; calculate the racket angle; guide your backswing in just the right way; time exactly when to start the forward swing; and contact the ball just the right way. You may be consciously *aware* of these things going on, but they are guided by a well-trained subconscious, that part of your brain that does things automatically.

A good example of this is tying your shoe. After doing it for years or decades, do you consciously guide each movement? No – your hands just fly about doing what they've done so many times that you no longer need to pay attention. You just watch and are aware of it as it is taking place. As an exercise, try tying your shoes except don't make any move until you've consciously chosen exactly what needs to be done, and do this each step of the way. See what happens?

Similarly, a properly trained table tennis player doesn't consciously guide his shots; he just watches as the subconscious does what it's done so many times before. Of course it's more complicated in table tennis since the ball is moving and spinning, unlike a stationary shoe, which is why it takes a lot of training to get right.

So what should your conscious mind be doing in a rally when training and playing a match? Here are five things it should be doing.

First, the conscious mind guides the training process. You have to decide what type of training the subconscious needs, and then train those skills. It should be analyzing what's going on and figuring out what changes are needed and what type of training needs to be done. But it should only be doing this between points.

Second, the conscious mind should be watching what happens. The subconscious can't see what's going on unless you are watching as well. So focus on what's going on. This primarily means watching the ball, but it also means watching the opponent to see what he does. The key is that you only watch, and let the trained subconscious react. This is the primary – and perhaps only – purpose of the conscious mind during a point. (You should also be listening to the sound of the ball as it hits the rackets and table, which helps with timing and reading the shot.)

Third, the conscious mind should remember the feel of a properly hit shot. (This might be the most important and least applied.) If you know the feel of a good smash or loop, you can essentially ask your subconscious to repeat that feel – and it'll usually oblige, assuming you've trained it well. When you miss a shot or the technique is wrong, the feel should be wrong, and you should focus on remembering what that proper feel should be – and your subconscious will get the message, and try to repeat it. Never focus on the shots that miss or that are wrong or your subconscious will begin to emulate those. (The only exception is if you absolutely cannot get it right, and have to consciously analyze what you are doing wrong – but there the goal is to get it right, and then focus on what is right, i.e. that right "feel.")

Fourth, the conscious mind chooses the basic tactics in a game situation. This should happen between points, never during a rally. This is easy when simply choosing what serve to do. It gets trickier when choosing tactics based on possible situations. For example, if you decide to attack the opponent's wide forehand, you have to wait for the right opportunity to do so. If you decide you need to attack the opponent's forehand, your subconscious will get the message, and when it sees a chance to attack, it'll attack the wide forehand. (Some believe they consciously make these decisions in a rally, but often it is the subconscious doing what the conscious mind has asked it to do, with the conscious mind simply being aware of it as it happens.) If you regularly think about tactics between points, the subconscious will get the message and will soon reflexively do these tactics at the proper times. At the advanced levels most tactics are reflexive. When a top player suddenly, say, tactically drops the ball short, he didn't consciously decide to do so; his trained subconscious saw the tactical opportunity and did so.

Five, the conscious mind needs to simply let go, both emotionally and in shot execution. An emotional mind will tend to interfere with shots, which is why professional athletes often look so bland just before and during rallies. A conscious mind that tries to take control will only interfere with the trained subconscious. So during a rally clear the mind and let go, and let the subconscious do what it's been trained to do.

So learn to work with your subconscious. Train it and let it go. In the end, it'll learn to execute, while you, the conscious part that's in charge, mostly just watches during actual play. You should almost feel guilty about this – you just stand around watching while the subconscious pulls off the shots, and guess who gets the credit?

June 8, 2015 – What to Think About in a Match

Have you ever been in a close match, began to think about winning and losing, and fell apart and lost? Or perhaps you were winning, began to think about it, and again fell apart and lost? It's almost certain that you have been in both scenarios. So how do you avoid this?

A key thing is to *have something else to think about.* The mind can only think about one thing at a time. As an experiment, try thinking about what serve you might use in a match against a specific player you play regularly, and see if you can think about winning and losing at the same time. You can't – in fact, the very thinking about what serve to do will likely wipe away most nervousness as nervousness comes from thinking (i.e. worrying) about winning and losing.

So give your mind something else to focus on. And that should be basic tactics. In theory you could think about anything else, but then you might not be paying attention to what's going on at the table, and you probably wouldn't play as well or as smart. But if you focus on basic tactics you get a double whammy – you play smarter table tennis, and you stop worrying about winning or losing. The key is to keep it simple; don't overthink. Focus on why you are winning – which serves, receives, and rally shots are winning points for you. Ask yourself:

- **Which serves are working for me?** This is the one time where you have complete control of the start of a rally, so take advantage of it. Focus on what to do with expected receives, but keep the mind clear and ready for anything.

- **What receives are working for me?** Focus on what to do with expected serves, but keep the mind clear and ready for anything.
- **What types of rallies are working for me?** Focus on the one or two most important things. It could be specific placements, a type of shot you want to use, or something as simple as "keep attacking." But again, keep the mind clear and ready for anything.

If you keep your mind on these basic tactics, then you'll keep your mind occupied so you won't think about winning or losing, which is a quick way to blow a match.

Here are a few additional tips:

- If you are winning and start thinking about it, perhaps convince yourself that you are losing. Reverse the score in your mind if necessary. Then think about what basic tactics are winning points for you, and focus on those.
- If you are "In the Zone," and playing extremely well, the worst thing you can do is think about it. If you do, just smile inwardly, and think of yourself as an observer watching while your body and subconscious perform. (But *you'll* get the credit!)
- If you do lose your focus in a contested game, that's when to take a time-out. Any time you lose focus you need to clear you mind, and then get it back on track, thinking about basic tactics and *nothing else.*

August 15, 2016 – How to Deal with Nervousness and Play Your Best: Magic, Best Match, Tactics

A player recently asked me how to deal with nervousness in a match. I've written articles on the topic, and there are a number of techniques for dealing with this – as I pointed out to the players, different methods work for different players. The player asked me, "What do *you* do?" And so here are my methods for dealing with nervousness – and it has a 100% success rate. I may not play well in a match, but I haven't had a problem with nervousness in many decades. Plus when I follow these three simple things, I almost always play my best. Here's my personal three-part technique.

1. I pretend my racket is a magic wand and I'm a magician. When I'm out there, I can do magic and make the ball do what I want it to do. I'll think of myself as Jan-Ove Waldner, who's often been called a magician at the table, and so I have complete faith I can do the same, whether I'm serving, receiving, or rallying.

2. I remember my best matches. Often I'll think back to perhaps the best match I ever played, when I beat Rey Domingo (2500 player), where the ball seemed to move in slow motion and everything I did worked – looping, smashing, blocking, receive, etc. – and I won easily. There was magic in that match, so all I have to do is recapture that magic and remember what it felt like.

3. I think about tactics. Your mind can't think about two things at the same time, so if I'm focused on tactics, I can't be nervous. Tactics is how you *apply* the magic from the two items above.

So, are you a magician? Have you had matches where you played great, the ball seemed to move in slow motion, and there was magic in the air? Are you focused on tactics when you play? This is what works for me.

October 11, 2016 – Taking the Shot Versus Letting it Happen

A common thinking problem when playing is thinking of an attacking shot as "going for a shot." This is a mistake – it leads to a deep-held belief that you are going for something risky and therefore inconsistent, which leaves you with a lack of confidence in the shot, which makes you hesitant, which leads to inconsistency.

Instead, think of any attacking shot as just another shot, no different than a push. You aren't "going for a shot," you are simply letting it happen by doing something you've probably done thousands of times before. If you haven't, then doing it a thousand times is your next assignment – it's called *practice*. Ideally, practice the shot with multiball training until it is so second nature that when it's time to do so in a real rally, it will still be second nature. Then do it in practice sessions with a partner, then practice games, and finally in real matches in tournaments or leagues.

Even if the shot is not yet second nature, you should still believe you will make it every time if you want to maximize your consistency.

Know that you can make any shot that you reasonably might try. Don't force a shot; just let the shots that you've practiced happen, and they will happen far more consistently than if you force them or think that you are "going for a shot."

There's a simple test of whether you have the right mentality when attacking. You should be *surprised* when you miss, because you should be so sure you can make the shot that any other outcome doesn't enter you mind, leading to that surprise if you miss.

All of this is true whether you are attacking consistently or trying to end the point. You aren't "going for a shot." You are simply doing what you trained to do, what you know you can do, and what you expect to do. And if you do happen to miss, just shake your head in disbelief, make the needed adjustment, and *know* that you'll never miss again.

July 7, 2014 – Playing Bad – It's All Mental (Usually)

When players play poorly, relative to their normal level of play, they usually attribute it by just saying they played poorly. That's circular reasoning – they played poorly because they played poorly? Actually, there's always a reason when you play poorly. And the reason is *almost always* mental.

I cannot emphasize this enough. Unless something is physical wrong with you or your equipment, or you are seriously out of practice, playing bad is *always* mental. Period. It's a simple concept that many don't get.

Is there something physically wrong with you? Don't say you are old or out of shape; these are constants that limit your playing level, but they don't make you play bad, relative to your normal level, since dealing with these factors is part of your normal level. No, something is physically wrong with you only if it's something that's not normal. Other common chronic problems that might lower your level include knee problems, back problems, sore arm, etc. But again, these do not make you play poorly; they simply lower your overall level of play. Maybe you were just tired? Well, that's a reason to play poorly; get more rest!

Is there something wrong with your equipment? This can happen, but it's rare. Usually it's your own fault. Is your rubber surface dirty and so not grabby as usual? Clean it. Is it getting old and so is losing its bounce? Get new sponge. (If you can't afford new sponge, then it's a chronic problem.) Is it humid? Keep a towel just for your racket and ball so you can keep them dry. I'll also include here other factors in the equipment category. I'm used to playing in near perfect conditions, and so when I play on slippery floors, on brown wood floors with orange balls (where the floor and ball are similarly colored, so I lose the ball in the background), or in bad lighting, I play poorly. Is this an equipment problem or a chronic problem? This might be classified as both. The fact that I don't play well in poor conditions is a chronic problem that lowers my overall level of play, but only in certain circumstances.

Are you out of practice? Whose fault is that? Solution: Go practice. If you don't have time to practice, then it's a chronic problem that simply lowers your overall level of play.

So if nothing is affecting your play physically, and you can't blame it on your equipment, and you are in practice, what can you blame your poor play on? Yes, it's all mental. There are so many ways a player can talk himself out of playing well. The most common is by harping on the poor shots instead of the good ones. Harp on the good ones, and you'll likely begin to emulate them. Harp on the bad ones, and that's what you'll continue to do since that's what you're thinking about, and the brain (i.e. the subconscious) tends to mimic what it is thinking about. Or perhaps you got nervous? Yep, that's all in your head. Or you got defensive when you had a lead? Another mental problem. Or you just weren't up to playing? Yep, that's mental.

I could go on and on, but the conclusion over and over is the same. When you play poorly, it's almost always mental. And guess what? With practice, you can get control over the mental aspect. You have to choose to do so, but once you do, you'll rarely have a bad day again.

CHAPTER EIGHT: EQUIPMENT

November 30, 2015 – Use Equipment that Matches the Way You Want to Play

Should one search for the perfect equipment that matches his game, or adjust his game to match his equipment? This is never an easy question, but here is the main factor to consider. Once you are beyond the beginning stage it's time to think long-term, and think about what your ultimate style of play will be. Once you decide that, look at some of the top players who play that style. What equipment are they using? If you want to play like them and hit shots like them, it's helpful to have similar equipment. So once you are past the beginning stage, it's time to adjust your equipment to *the way you want to play.*

The comparison isn't exact; they play at a much higher level and train full-time (including physical training), so depending on your level, you might want something slower, though not too much so. For example, if their sponge is too fast, you might want a slower version.

One other thing to take into consideration is that if your game is centered around looping – as nearly all players at the higher levels are – then you do want something extra bouncy, that allows you to loop nearly anything, in particular one of the tensored sponges.

April 25, 2016 – Clean Your Racket

It's a simple concept – keep your inverted sponge rubber clean!!! It doesn't take much play for the surface to gather dust and lose some of its grippiness. It may not seem like much since it's a gradual process, but it really can make a difference – though often players don't notice it. (Related to this is that you should get new sponge periodically – the surface wears down and the sponge gradually loses its bounciness. Since I play 6-7 days/week, I change both sides every month; others who don't play as much may go six months or even a year, though the latter is a bit long if you want to have lively, spinny shots.) Here's my three-part recommendation:

- Wash it off with water before every session. The simplest way is to wet a corner of a towel (and you do have a towel when you play to wipe away sweat and clean your racket, right?), and wipe it off with that. Then wipe the water away and dry the racket with a dry part of the towel.
- A few times each game simply breathe on the sponge's surface, and then wipe it on your pants or towel. This gets rid of gathering dust.
- At the start of serious competitions, and perhaps once a week otherwise, use rubber cleaner to really clean it off.

December 24, 2016 – Ask the Distributor!

At clubs all across the nation and the world, the same routine goes on all the time – players are constantly asking and talking about equipment. Only ratings are more discussed. (Typical greeting at a club: "What's your rating? What equipment do you use?") And it's true that you can learn a lot by asking others about equipment – and better still, trying out their equipment.

But think about it – a distributor might have dozens of sponges and dozens of rackets that might suit your game. The possible combinations can run into the thousands. While you may gain valuable information asking questions, remember that they mostly know what works for *them*, and no two players play alike. You need to find what works for *you*. You may find this by experimenting, but the probability that someone else at the club just happens to have the perfect racket and sponge combination for you isn't likely.

But there's an expert out there ready to help – and that's the equipment expert at the distributor. All of the major ones have someone like this, who has literally tried out every combination of their equipment, and knows just about all there is to know about all of them. Their job is to find a perfect combination for you – because if they don't, you'll be going to a rival. Not only that, but each of these distributor "equipment junkies" lives and breathes table tennis equipment, and so it will be his lifelong dream to discuss your equipment needs and find you the perfect combination. He'll know what questions to ask of your game with the goal of finding you just what you need.

So if you aren't sure yet about what equipment to use, why not contact one of the major distributors and *ASK*? (You can also find a distributor at most major tournaments.)

CHAPTER NINE: TOURNAMENTS

October 20, 2014 – Top Ten Ways to Play Your Best in a Tournament

1) Put together a list of tips for yourself.

For example, you might write down "Stay low" if you tend to stand up too straight. Or you might write, "Relax and have fun." You should refer to this list periodically during the tournament.

2) Decide what your mental frame of mind should be.

Some players get too hyped up for their matches, and so don't play well. Others can't get up for their matches, and also don't play well. Decide where you stand in this spectrum, and either calm yourself down or psyche yourself up before each match. Decide in advance what you need to do. You might prepare differently for each match, based on the opponent's playing style. If you anticipate that you will have to be more aggressive against one opponent, you might have to be more "psyched up" for that match. On the other hand, being hyped up might only make you miss more. You have to decide what works for you.

3) Work on specific strengths and weaknesses.

Everyone has specific strengths and weaknesses that many of their matches are won or lost on. Decide what these shots are, and make sure to practice them both before and during the tournament. For example, if you have trouble with a specific serve, have someone serve it to you over and over – even if you have to pay someone to do it! Similarly, if you have a big strength, such as a forehand smash, make sure to get it going BEFORE the match begins, not when you've already dug yourself a hole by missing the first five attempts.

4) Decide what your actual and working goals are.

For most people, the actual goal is to win. This doesn't mean you aren't there to have fun, but ultimately, most people are trying to win. However, if you go out to a match with this in mind, you might not play your best – you'll be too nervous. Instead, have a "working goal," i.e. a goal that will maximize your chances of winning. Generally, make "playing your best" your working goal. If you play your best, your chances of winning are maximized, right? You may vary this, however; if you tend to play too passively, for example, your working goal might be to play aggressively.

5) Arrange a warm-up partner and practice routine in advance.

The night before the tournament, arrange who you will warm up with and when. Pick someone who you are comfortable warming up with. This is not the time to practice against someone whose game gives you trouble, or plays what seems to you a "weird" style – that's what you should have been practicing against at the club in the weeks before the tournament. On the day of the tournament, you want someone who can help you groove your shots, not just whoever happens to be available – so arrange this in advance. Once your shots are grooved and warmed up, you can then adjust to the many wacky styles you may face (as well as more standard ones). Decide in advance what drills you want to do; don't just do forehand to forehand, etc. – make sure to do footwork drills and serve & receive drills. Make sure to either play out points or play some games before you go out for your tournament match – you don't want the first real points you play to be in a tournament match.

6) Bring food & beverages, and eat lightly.

Good food & beverage services at tournament sites are rare. Drink water or bring your own drinks (Gatorade, for example), as well as snacks (such as fruit). Avoid eating a large meal during the tournament unless you have two hours or more free afterwards. It's best to snack regularly on easily digested food (mostly carbohydrates), or you will be somewhat tired while you digest the large meal.

7) Prepare for slippery floors.

One of the most common mistakes I see is not preparing for a slippery floor. Over half of tournaments are played on flooring that is not grippy enough for you to play your best. Many players don't even realize how much they are giving up until they do something about it – and their playing level shoots up. What can you do? There are several options. First, make sure you have good, grippy shoes. Some players even bring two pairs of shoes – one normal pair, and one "extra grippy' for slippery floors. Second, you should always bring a small towel or paper towels to a tournament. If the floors are slippery, dampen the towel, and put it to the side of the table. Every few points, rub your feet on them. Try this, and you'll find it makes a huge difference.

8) Practice your serves.

The day of the tournament, practice your serves. Tuning them up will pay off more for you, time-for-time, than just about any other practice. Yet most players don't warm up their serves before a match, and so don't have their best serves available.

9) Prepare physically.

Prepare your muscles for combat! Before warming up at the table, do some easy jogging to get them warm. Do a thorough stretching routine. Finally, before each match, you might do some short but vigorous physical activity to get the muscles prepared. You might shadow practice, or do a few sprints; however, make sure not to tire yourself out so much that you can't play the match. Somewhat related to this is getting enough sleep in the last few days before the tournament. (I've read studies that have shown that it's actually more important getting enough sleep in the last few days before a sports activity than the actual night before.)

10) Do some meditation and mental visualization.

Let's not get mystical here. However, you will play better if you take some time before a match to clear your mind and do some mental visualization. Go somewhere quiet, and blank your mind out. Then visualize yourself doing the shots you plan on doing. A few minutes of this is worth more than an equal amount of practice time on the table.

December 31, 2016 – Top Ten Ways to Win and Lose a Match

Top Ten Ways to Win a Match

1. Come into the match physically and mentally prepared
2. Have a solid game plan, or quickly develop one
3. Dominate with serves
4. Control play with receive
5. Get your strengths into play
6. Dominate with quickness or power
7. Consistency
8. Placement and depth
9. Variation
10. Mental grit

Top Ten Ways to Lose a Match

1. See above. Add "Do not" or "Poor" at the start of each.

March 7, 2016 – Preparing for Major Events – a Checklist

Players often come unprepared at tournaments and leagues. Here's a quick checklist of things to prepare in advance of the event. (Some of this was covered in previous Tips, but this gives you an actual checklist, with a few new items.)

- **Lighting and Backgrounds**. You are likely used to the lighting and backgrounds at your table tennis club, but when you go to a tournament or league at a different venue, you have to adjust to the new conditions. Show up early so you can warm up at the new venue to get used to the lighting and backgrounds – and note that "backgrounds" is pluralized as you should try to move around a bit and get used to different backgrounds. Often this means just switching sides on the table you are practicing on, since often one side looks onto the wall at the side of the gym, the other into the vast expanse of the gym – two very different backgrounds to adjust to.

- **Floors**. If you play with good, grippy floors, then you'll likely have problems if you have to compete on slippery ones. Surprisingly, it works the other way too – if you are used to slippery floors in practice, playing on grippy ones might give you trouble as you are used to sliding your feet across the floor as you move. So come early to adjust to the floors. If you are used to grippy floors, then bring grippy shoes to help adjust to slippery ones.

- **Tables and Balls**. Different types do play different, so do try to practice in advance on the tables and balls you will be using. You might want to order a few of each major type of ball so you'll always be prepared for this. If your club doesn't have the same type of table as the event you are going to, then come in early at the event to practice on theirs.

- **Towel**. Especially if it's summer and you are used to playing in air conditioning, and you get caught playing in a non-air conditioned venue, you will want a towel, to wipe away sweat both on you, your racket, and the ball. Always keep a towel in your playing bag – *Hitchhiker's Guide to the Galaxy* was right about this. (Google it.)

- **Food and Drinks**. Don't risk having to eat the local food and drinks unless you know in advance what will be there. You can usually assume there'll be plain water, but other than that you might want to either bring your own food and drinks, or investigate in advance what will be locally available.

- **Warm-up Partner**. You should arrange someone in advance. Let's face it, some players are easy to warm up with, others are not. Tournaments and leagues are not the time to experiment with how you warm up; arrange this in advance with someone you are familiar and comfortable warming up with.

- **Serve and Receive**. Why do so many players forget to practice their serves before a major event? They practice everything else, but forget this. You might also want to find a partner and practice receive.

- **Sports Psychology**. If you come in nervous, you are handicapping yourself. So make sure to come in with a positive attitude, ready to confidently take on the world!

September 28, 2015 – Watch the Top Players Before a Tournament or Big Match

One of the best ways to play your best is to watch the top players. Their techniques and timing will rub off on you. Your subconscious, which really controls your play, will especially pick up on it. Choose a top player who has a similar game and strokes, and just imagine being that player as you watch. Focus on:

- their strokes;
- their consistency;
- how they move;
- how they serve to set up their shots;
- how they receive to stop the server from making a strong attack;
- how focused they are.

Just remember not to over-play. What looks like a big shot from a top player is often just an average shot for them. Focus on their techniques, tactics, mental strength, and consistency.

March 9, 2015 – Playing in Poor Conditions

Playing a tournament in absolutely perfect conditions is like that mythical annual vacation at the beach where everything goes perfect. But life is not a beach vacation, and neither is table tennis. You not only should be prepared for poor conditions, but as players, you should *expect* them (and be happy when the conditions are good). This doesn't mean you should just accept bad conditions; by all means work to make sure tournament and club directors have great conditions. But as players you have to adapt to the playing environment. Tactical players adapt; non-tactical players complain. Here's a short primer:

- **Slippery floors.** If your club has great floors, there's nothing more frustrating than showing up at a tournament primed to play like greased lightning, only to find you're playing on a skating rink. Most major tournaments are played on concrete or wood floors, and unless they are treated properly, they will be slippery. So what can you do?

    First, have a good pair of table tennis shoes. They are designed to give the best possible traction. Make sure to have a new pair as worn-out ones won't give as much traction. Many players who play at clubs with good floors get lazy on this, letting their shoes wear out, and don't realize this until they are stuck on slippery floors. I suggest getting news ones for such tournaments, and use them only when needed, until the ones you use in practice are falling apart.

Second, step on a wet cloth between points. Watch the top players and you'll see this all the time if they aren't playing on good floors. It can be a wet paper towel or a cloth, it doesn't matter. You'll get much better traction after stepping on it for several points.

Third, use it to your advantage. Players can't move as well on slippery floors, so move your opponents around!

- **Poor lighting or background**. There's only one good answer here – adjust. You do this by practicing. One common mistake is that sometimes only one side has a bad background. So make sure to practice on both sides of the table, and on any tables you might play on that might have bad backgrounds. You might also want to start the match on the "good" side, so you don't have to both adapt to your opponent and the conditions at the same time.

   And once again, use it to your advantage. If the lighting or background is poor, it's harder for players to follow the ball. This favors attackers, since defenders are trying to pick up on a fast-moving ball. This doesn't mean wild attacks, but when it's harder to see, play a bit more aggressively, and expect shorter rallies.

- **Bad tables, balls, or a breeze**. This means the ball is going to take funny hops, or move about in the breeze. It's going to be difficult to play well, so accept that. Rallies will tend to be short, and will favor the player who focuses on consistency. This doesn't mean completely changing your game, but focus on keeping the ball in play and letting the opponent make mistakes off the erratic movement of the ball. (Note – there are generally two types of "bad" tables – ones with slippery surfaces, where the ball slides, and ones where the ball dies when it hits near the side-lines or end-lines. Good tables have tops that are thick enough – usually one inch – so the ball bounces consistently all over the surface.)

193

- **Humidity**. There's nothing more frustrating than doing that perfect loop you've done ten thousand times before, and the ball slides off your racket into the net. When it's humid, both the ball and racket can get damp, and it'll change the characteristics of how the ball comes off your racket. How do you combat this?

  First, make sure to have a dry towel to dry your racket and the ball off with. If you sweat a lot, you should bring two towels, one for you, one for the racket and ball. Then use the towel(s) a lot, making sure the racket, ball, and your hands are dry. (A wet non-playing hand means the ball gets wet; a wet playing hand means you can't grip the racket very well.)

  Second, adapt tactically. You won't be able to overpower an opponent with spin, so loopers have to either go to more drive loops (sinking the ball into the sponge, and so less spin, more speed, not as consistent), or steady loops where you mostly keep the rally going. Hitters and blockers have the advantage here, so you might do more of that – but often they too have problems with the humidity as it changes the friction on their racket, and so they block loops into the net. One of the most successful ways to play in humid conditions against a looper is to simply dead block over and over, and watch the poor looper try to loop with any effectiveness.

- **Cold**. I've seen many players in the winter struggle in their early matches because their racket is cold – and they often don't even notice it. Or they aren't warmed up because their racket was cold when they were warming up, and now that the racket is warmer, it's playing different than it was when they were warming up. A cold racket plays deader. So if you are driving to a tournament and it's cold outside, keep your racket inside the car with you, not in the trunk where it'll get cold.

Finally, a reminder – when faced with bad conditions, you can either surrender to them and lose, or take advantage of them and win. Save the complaining for when you aren't playing, which usually means *after* the tournament is done.

October 6, 2014 – Should You Play Tournaments When Working on Something New?

To improve you need both good technique and match experience. You can get match experience at a club, but you get a lot more in tournaments, where you play new players and find out where your game really stands – feedback that helps you pinpoint what you need to work on. The question is what to do when you are working on new techniques. If you play tournaments – or matches, for that matter – you'll likely fall back into your old habits, and re-enforce them. So sometimes it's better to skip tournaments and matches for a time while you work on the new techniques.

But how long should you skip them? There's an easy measure. When you are changing techniques, it's best not to play matches – practice or tournaments – until you've mastered the new technique to the point where you'll reflexively use it in matches. This doesn't mean you should skip playing matches until the technique is perfect and you never get it wrong, but it means waiting until you can do it in a match situation most of the time. Otherwise you'll just be re-enforcing bad habits.

By playing matches when the technique is almost perfected, but not quite, you'll re-enforce your ability to do it under pressure – and that's half the problem with developing a new technique. In fact, the best measure of whether you have learned the new technique is to see if you use it not only under match pressure, but under the intense pressure of a close match. If you can do it at deuce, you can do it anytime.

A famous example of skipping tournaments and matches in general was Hungary's Istvan Jonyer. He made the Hungarian National Team in the early 1970s mostly by blocking. While on the team he developed his powerful forehand loop and became Hungarian National Champion. But he had a weak backhand, and couldn't really compete with the best players in the world. Then he spent six months up in a mountain training, where he did essentially nothing but backhand loop. He didn't play matches as he worked on this. When he finished, he had a great backhand loop – though other aspects of his game had deteriorated, and he had to practice them to get them back. About two years later he became the 1975 Men's World Champion, and was #1 in the world for two years and a dominant top ten (usually top five) player for over a decade.

195

So take a look at your game, and decide what techniques you need to fix. Then decide if it's worth spending a lot of time fixing them while skipping matches. In the short run it can be frustrating, as you are just dying to play matches. In the long run it'll pay off.

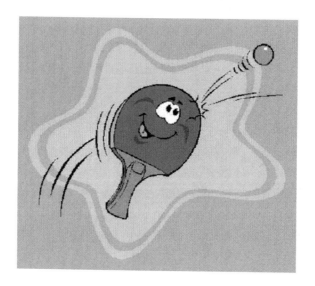

ABOUT THE AUTHOR

USA Table Tennis Hall of Famer Larry Hodges has spent most of the past 25 years coaching at the Maryland Table Tennis Center (www.mdttc.com) in Gaithersburg, Maryland, along with co-coaches Cheng Yinghua, Jack Huang, and numerous others. He is certified as a National Coach, the highest level of coaching certification in USA Table Tennis, as well as an ITTF Coach. He maintains the coaching site TableTennisCoaching.com, with numerous coaching articles, videos, and his daily table tennis blog.

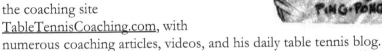

He's the chair of the USATT's Coaching Committee and a two-time USATT Coach of the Year. In 2007 he won the USATT President's Award. He has been the match coach for over 200 Junior Olympic and Junior National gold medalists, more than any other USA table tennis coach. He has worked with many of the best players in the country, both in Maryland and as manager and later a director and coach at the Olympic Training Center from 1985-1989. For many years he coached the U.S. National Junior Team at tournaments in the U.S. and around the world, including third place at the 1994 World Youth Cup Championships in Taiwan.

As of March, 2017, he was the author of over 1700 published articles in over 150 different publications, including over 1500 on table tennis, over half of them coaching articles. He has eight books on table tennis. (See next page.)

Larry began playing table tennis in 1976 at age 16. He has been ranked among the top 20 players in the U.S. and has won state championships in Maryland, Colorado and North Carolina. He was U.S. National Collegiate Doubles and two-time National Team Champion for the University of Maryland, where he received a bachelor's degree in Math and a master's degree in Journalism. Although he normally uses sponge, he also has 19 national titles in hardbat table tennis – U.S. Nationals and U.S. Open Singles Champion, 13-times National or Open Doubles Champion, and 4-time Over 40 Champion.

When he's not coaching, playing, or writing about table tennis, Larry enjoys reading and writing science fiction and fantasy—he's a member of Science Fiction Writers of America, with over 80 short story sales and four novels.

Table Tennis Books by Larry Hodges

See tabletenniscoaching.com or direct from Amazon.com.

Table Tennis Tactics for Thinkers	Table Tennis Tales & Techniques
Best-selling table tennis book!	Essays on technique and tales of the sport — the funny & interesting side.

Table Tennis Tips	More Table Tennis Tips
150 tips, all in one volume.	150 more tips, all in one volume.

Table Tennis: Steps to Success
The Fundamentals of Table Tennis. Over 30,000 copies sold in six languages; new version planned.

Professional Table Tennis Coaches Handbook
How to be a professional coach.

Instructor's Guide to Table Tennis
How to coach, and the USATT coaching manual for many years! (Currently out of print.)

The Spirit of Pong
A fantasy table tennis novel where an American goes to China to learn the secrets of table tennis, and trains with the spirits of past champions.

And don't forget to check out Larry's daily table tennis blog:
www.TableTennisCoaching.com

Made in the USA
Middletown, DE
30 August 2024

60042775R00113